The Complete Guide to

SARBANES-OXLEY

Understanding How Sarbanes-Oxley
Affects Your Business

STEPHEN M. BAINBRIDGE

Adams Business
Avon, Massachusetts

Published by Adams Media, an F+W Publications Company
57 Littlefield Street
Avon, MA 02322
www.adamsmedia.com

ISBN 10: 1-59869-267-4
ISBN13: 978-1-59869-267-9

J   I   H   G   F   E   D   C   B   A

Printed in the United States of America

Library of Congress Cataloging-in-Publication Data
Bainbridge, Stephen M.
The complete guide to Sarbanes-Oxley / Stephen M. Bainbridge.
p.   cm.
Includes index.
ISBN-13: 978-1-59869-267-9 (pbk.)
ISBN-10: 1-59869-267-4 (pbk.)

1. Corporations—Accounting—Law and legislation—
United States. 2. Disclosure of information—Law and legislation—
United States. 3. Financial statements—Law and legislation—United States.
4. Corporate governance—Law and legislation—United States.
5. Auditing, Internal—Law and legislation—United States.
6. United States. Sarbanes-Oxley Act of 2002. I. Title.
KF1446.Z9B35 2007
346.73'0666—dc22 2007002036

This publication is designed to provide accurate and authoritative information with regard to the subject matter covered. It is sold with the understanding that the publisher is not engaged in rendering legal, accounting, or other
professional advice. If legal advice or other expert assistance is required, the
services of a competent professional person should be sought.
—From a *Declaration of Principles* jointly adopted by a Committee of the
American Bar Association and a Committee of Publishers and Associations

Many of the designations used by manufacturers and sellers to distinguish
their product are claimed as trademarks. Where those designations appear in
this book and Adams Media was aware of a trademark claim, the designations
have been printed with initial capital letters.

This book is available at quantity discounts for bulk purchases.
For information, please call 1-800-289-0963.

CONTENTS

INTRODUCTION

As the Sarbanes-Oxley Act approaches age five, it's appropriate to look back at how the act has affected American businesses and also to look forward to assess future trends. After all, the Sarbanes-Oxley Act had the biggest impact on American business of any federal securities legislation since the New Deal.

Understanding how Sarbanes-Oxley works and the demands it makes on corporations is especially critical for directors and managers of smaller public corporations. Until recently, the smallest public corporations have been partially insulated from the full costs of complying with the act by rules of the Securities and Exchange Commission (the SEC, sometimes referred to as "the Commission") that defer full application of SOX to such firms. The SEC has announced, however, that this limited regulatory relief will be coming to an end within the next two years. Accordingly, it appears that all public corporations will be required to fully comply with Sarbanes-Oxley by 2008.

To be sure, when the SEC announced in December 2006 its guidance for how smaller public corporations should comply with the most expensive provision of SOX, the media widely reported that the Commission had provided significant regulatory relief for smaller public corporations. In fact, however, we'll see that the relief offered by the SEC's guidance is more cosmetic than real. In addition, the SEC's Director of the Division of Corporation Finance issued a press release stating that that the new guidance was not intended to replace existing procedures already in place at companies, "provided of course that those meet the standards of Section 404 and our rules."

Managers and directors of small public corporations thus now face the same questions SOX has long posed for the largest companies: How do they comply with SOX? How does SOX affect relations within the firm? Should the company go private in order to avoid the need to comply with SOX? A practical guide to SOX basics thus could not be more timely.

Who Should Read This Book?

This book was written with four audiences in mind:

- Directors and managers of large public corporations, whose firms have been required to fully comply with SOX from the outset. If you're one of these directors and/or managers, this book provides you with a five-year update on how SOX has been implemented and some advice to help you with your ongoing compliance efforts.
- Directors and managers of small public corporations, whose firms are only now being required to fully comply with SOX. What should you expect during the first year the law applies to you? Should you really consider going dark and avoiding the need for SOX compliance altogether?
- Directors and managers of closely held corporations who are considering taking their companies public. What additional obligations will SOX impose on you following an initial public offering (IPO), and what costs are you likely to face? How can those costs be minimized?
- Directors and managers of larger closely held corporations and nonprofit entities, whose corporations are not obliged to comply with SOX but choose to voluntarily comply. In such situations, how can you adapt to SOX in a way that fits your needs?

This is not a book aimed at lawyers or accountants. I don't want you to get bogged down in legal or accounting technicalities. Rather, it is a nontechnical, "plain English" guide for the managers and directors of the 13,000 or so publicly held corporations subject to Sarbanes-Oxley, as well as the managers and directors of the thousands of large closely held corporations considering raising capital via an IPO (which would subject them to SOX) or otherwise facing market pressures to at least partially comply with SOX.

Given that SOX brought about the most significant changes in corporate governance and securities regulation since the 1930s, businesspeople need to have the law and its requirements explained simply and practically. In addition to explaining key legal provisions in the legislation, of course, *The Complete Guide to Sarbanes-Oxley* also provides an overview of best practices and business policies.

To be sure, there will be many points in the Sarbanes-Oxley compliance process at which the legal complexities will be sufficiently challenging that, as a director or manager, you will need to talk to a lawyer or to an accountant. I'll flag those areas.

In sum, if you've found yourself asking such questions as "What does SOX mean to me now? Do I have to worry about it? How much legal help do I need? How much accounting help do I need? What information technology requirements will we face?"—then this book will give you the practical, nontechnical answers that you need.

Before we begin, a few personal notes. I wish to thank my agent, Edward Claflin, and my editors at Adams Media, Shoshanna Grossman and Richard Wallace. I especially thank my wife, Helen, for her support, her careful editing of the text, and her many helpful suggestions.

1

The Sarbanes-Oxley Act: How We Got Here, and What It Means

The opening years of this decade were not kind to Wall Street. The stock market ended the year lower three years running in 2000 to 2002, which was the first time there had been three down years in a row since the 1930s. It wasn't just a weak economy that was pounding the market, however. It seemed like every week brought new reports of misdeeds at leading American corporations and financial institutions. The now infamous scandal at Enron turned out not to be an isolated case, as news of corporate shenanigans at companies like WorldCom, Global Crossing, Tyco, Adelphia, and others soon followed.

We soon learned that the rot extended far beyond the corporate executive suite. New York Attorney General Eliot Spitzer launched an investigation into conflicts of interest on the part of stock market analysts. Spitzer also turned up problems at many large mutual funds. And the beat went on.

By mid-2002, Congress decided it was past time to clean house. In July, it passed the "Public Company Accounting Reform and Investor Protection Act" of 2002—popularly known as the Sarbanes-Oxley Act, or SOX. When President George W. Bush signed the act later that month, he praised it for making "the most far-reaching reforms of American business practices since the time of Franklin Delano Roosevelt."

1

Those reforms include:

- The creation of the Public Company Accounting Oversight Board to oversee the accounting profession
- A number of mandates requiring companies to adopt more effective internal controls—i.e., the processes the company uses to ensure the reliability of its public financial disclosures and to make sure that it complies with applicable laws and regulations
- A requirement that the chief executive officer and chief financial officer of a company must certify its financial statements and disclosure reports
- A number of rules designed to ensure that a company's auditor is truly independent of company management
- A related requirement that companies have an audit committee consisting of independent directors to deal with the auditor and oversee the company's financial processes.
- New restrictions on loans to insiders and stock trading by insiders
- Changes in rules governing how corporations disclose information to the public, so as to increase the speed and transparency of such disclosures
- Protections for whistle blowers and restrictions on document destruction, designed to prevent the sort of obstruction of justice witnessed at Enron
- New and severe criminal and civil penalties for corporate misconduct

These reforms benefit the American economy in a number of ways, including restored investor confidence in the integrity of the capital markets, enhanced corporate disclosures, and reduced incentives for corporate management to manipulate stock prices.

Unfortunately, Sarbanes-Oxley also imposes a much higher regulatory burden on U.S. public corporations than the law's sponsors ever imagined. According to the *Wall Street Journal*, for example, publicly traded U.S. corporations routinely report that their audit costs have gone up as much as 30 percent, or even more, due to the tougher audit and accounting standards imposed by SOX. Indeed, just paying the fees now required to fund the Public Company Accounting Oversight Board (PCAOB) can run as much as $2 million a year for the largest firms.

WHO ARE SARBANES AND OXLEY?

In 1976, Paul Sarbanes was elected to the first of his five six-year terms as a Democratic senator from Maryland. In 2002, he was chairman of the Senate Banking, Housing, and Urban Affairs Committee, which had primary responsibility for developing the legislation that became SOX.

Michael G. Oxley become a Republican member of the House of Representatives from Ohio as the result of a 1981 special election; he was subsequently re-elected for twelve full two-year terms. In 2002, he was chairman of the House Financial Services Committee, which oversees Wall Street, banks, and the insurance industry, and he had primary responsibility for SOX on the House side.

Both Sarbanes and Oxley retired from Congress at the end of 2006.

Professional surveys of U.S. corporations confirm the *Journal*'s report. Foley & Lardner, a law firm that has conducted a number of empirical analyses of SOX and its impact on American business, found that senior managers of public middle-market companies expect costs directly associated with being public to increase by almost 100 percent as a result of increased disclosure and new corporate governance compliance rules imposed by SOX, new Securities and Exchange Commission (SEC) regulations, and changes to stock exchange listing requirements.

The Cost of Compliance

The chief regulatory culprit in the Sarbanes-Oxley Act is SOX § 404, which requires inclusion of internal control disclosures in each public corporation's annual report. This disclosure statement must include: (1) a written confirmation by which firm management acknowledges its responsibility for establishing and maintaining a system of internal controls and procedures for financial reporting; (2) an assessment, as of the end of the most recent fiscal year, of the effectiveness of the firm's internal controls; and (3) a written attestation by the firm's outside auditor confirming the adequacy and accuracy of those controls and procedures.

The SEC initially estimated § 404 compliance would require only 383 staff hours per company per year. According to a Financial Executives International survey of 321 companies, however, firms with greater than $5 billion in revenues spend an average of $4.7 million per year to comply with § 404. The survey also projected expenditures of 35,000 staff hours—almost 100 times the SEC's estimate. Finally, the survey estimated that firms will spend $1.3 million on external consultants and software and an extra $1.5 million (a jump of 35 percent) in audit fees.

In fairness, some of these costs were one-time expenses incurred to bring firms' internal controls up to snuff. Yet, many other SOX compliance costs recur year after year. For example, the internal control process required by § 404 relies heavily on ongoing documentation. As a result, firms must constantly ensure that they are creating the requisite paper trail.

Other ongoing expenses include legal fees, directors and officers (D&O) insurance policy premium increases, and the need to pay higher director fees in order to attract qualified independent directors to serve on boards of directors.

These costs are disproportionately borne by smaller public firms. A study by three University of Georgia economists, for example, found that post-SOX director compensation increases have been much higher at small firms:

> [S]mall firms paid $5.91 to non-employee directors on every $1,000 in sales in the pre-SOX period, which increased to $9.76 on every $1000 in sales in the post-SOX period. In contrast, large firms incurred 13 cents in director cash compensation per $1,000 in sales in the Pre-SOX period, which increased only to 15 cents in the Post-SOX period.

Likewise, a study by ARC Morgan found that companies with annual sales of less than $250 million incurred $1.56 million in external-resource costs simply to comply with one SOX provision (the internal controls required by § 404). Note that this figure includes internal costs, opportunity costs, and intangibles. In contrast, firms with annual sales of $1 to $2 billion incurred an average of $2.4 million in such costs.

In sum, SOX compliance weighs disproportionately on small public corporations. For many of these firms, the additional cost is a significant percentage of their annual revenues. For those firms operating on thin margins, SOX compliance costs can actually make the difference between profitability and losing money.

These costs have substantially distorted corporate financing decisions. On the one hand, SOX has discouraged privately held corporations from going public. As law professor Larry Ribstein observed on his blog (*www.ideoblog.com*), start-up "companies are opting for financing from private-equity firms," rather than using an IPO to raise money from the capital markets. In the long run, or perhaps the not-so-long run, this barrier to the public capital markets may have a very negative effect on the economy, according to Ribstein: "since going public is an important venture capital exit strategy, partially closing the exit could impede start-up financing, and therefore make it harder to get ideas off the ground."

At the same time, a Foley & Lardner survey found that 21 percent of responding publicly held corporations were considering going private in response to SOX. Law professor William Carney confirmed this result, finding that of 114 companies going private in 2004, 44 specifically cited SOX compliance costs as one of the reasons they were doing so. Ribstein summarizes the situation by noting: "There is evidence that SOX [has] an effect in causing firms to eliminate or reduce public ownership. . . . There is also evidence that firms with higher audit fees were more likely to go dark, thereby linking this decision with the costs of complying with SOX."

Unfortunately, the prospects for relief are dim. An SEC advisory committee tasked with assessing the impact of SOX and other securities laws on small public corporations released its final report on April 23, 2006. In that report, the committee concluded that the costs imposed on smaller public corporations by a number of key SOX provisions significantly exceeded any benefit those provisions provide investors.

In particular, the committee focused on SOX § 404, explaining that

[f]rom the earliest stages of its implementation, Sarbanes-Oxley Act § 404 has posed special challenges for smaller public companies. To some extent, the problems smaller companies have in complying with § 404 are the problems of companies generally:

- lack of clear guidance;
- an unfamiliar regulatory environment;
- an unfriendly legal and enforcement atmosphere that diminishes the use and acceptance of professional judgment because of fears of second-guessing by regulators and the plaintiffs bar;
- a focus on detailed control activities by auditors; and
- the lack of sufficient resources and competencies in an area in which companies and auditors have previously placed less emphasis.

But because of their different operating structures, smaller public companies have felt the effects of § 404 in a manner different from their larger counterparts. With more limited resources, fewer internal personnel and less revenue with which to offset both implementation costs and the disproportionate fixed costs of § 404 compliance, these companies have been disproportionately subject to the burdens associated with § 404 compliance.

Accordingly, the committee gave highest priority to a set of recommendations that would create a system of "scaled" securities regulation under which the smallest public corporations would be subject to less extensive disclosure and auditing requirements. In particular, the committee recommended that the SEC exempt the smallest public corporations from SOX § 404, so long as they have a qualified audit committee and have adopted a qualifying code of ethics for disclosure and audit practices.

On May 17, 2006, the SEC responded by—to be blunt—tossing the advisory committee report in the circular file. Instead of even considering the committee's detailed recommendations, which went well beyond just the narrow problems created by § 404, the SEC announced a modest set of regulatory actions limited solely to § 404 issues. Even within those narrow confines, moreover, the SEC's plans are surprisingly lame. In sum, the May 2006 announcement contemplated that small public corporations would get an extension on the date by which they are required to be fully compliant with § 404. "It is anticipated that any such postponement would nonetheless require all filers to comply with the management assessment required by Section 404(a) of Sarbanes-Oxley for fiscal years beginning on or after Dec. 16, 2006." Further, subject to SEC oversight, the Public Company Accounting Oversight Board (PCAOB) would amend its auditing standards so as to provide new guidance that would help reduce compliance costs by focusing auditor attention on "areas that pose higher risk of fraud or material error." Unlike the recommendations made by its own advisory committee, which would have provided significant and comprehensive regulatory relief for smaller public corporations, the SEC thus took a narrow and trivial approach to the problem.

In August 2006, however, the SEC issued a new statement backtracking on the hard line taken in May. One proposal made in the August announcement would give smaller firms until their fiscal year ending on or after December 15, 2008, to become fully SOX-compliant. (Note that because the firms will have to be SOX-compliant for that fiscal year, it actually means that some will have to start the SOX-compliance process in December 2007.) A second proposal would exempt newly public companies from having to be fully compliant with SOX until the company files its second annual report with the SEC. In December 2006, both proposals were adopted.

THE STATUTORY TEXT

We'll excerpt relevant portions of Sarbanes-Oxley as we go along. If you want the entire text of the statute in one place, you can download it from *www.sec.gov/about/laws/soa2002.pdf*. (Before you hit the "Print" button on this document, by the way, note that the statute itself runs longer than sixty pages.) A useful related resource is the collection of SEC announcements of rules and other actions taken pursuant to Sarbanes-Oxley, which is available online from the SEC at *www.sec.gov/spotlight/sarbanes-oxley.htm*.

Also in December 2006, both the SEC and PCAOB followed up on the May 2006 promise to provide additional guidance as to how companies should comply with Section 404. In so doing, however, the SEC continued to insist that "it is impractical to prescribe a single methodology that meets the needs of every company." As a result, the SEC declined to create safe harbors by which compliant firms are insulated from liability. Indeed, the SEC decided not even to "provide a checklist of steps management should perform in completing its evaluation" of the company's internal controls.

Instead, the SEC offered the following guidance:

Management should implement and conduct an evaluation that is sufficient to provide it with a reasonable basis for its annual assessment. Management should use its own experience and informed judgment in designing an evaluation process that aligns with the operations, financial reporting risks and processes of the company. If the evaluation process identifies material weaknesses that exist as of the end of the fiscal year, such weaknesses must be disclosed in management's annual report with a statement that ICFR [i.e., internal controls over financial reporting] is ineffective. If the evaluation identifies no internal control deficiencies that constitute a material weakness, management assesses ICFR as effective.

Management is required to assess as of the end of the fiscal year whether the company's ICFR is effective in providing reasonable assurance regarding the reliability of financial reporting. (From SEC Management's Report on Internal Control Over Financial Reporting, available at www.sec.gov/rules/proposed/2006/33-8762.pdf.)

The SEC's guidance is inherently vague and ambiguous, leaving plenty of room for interpretation and disagreement. Terms like "reasonable" and "material" are standards, which by their very nature fail to offer brightlines between lawful and unlawful consequence. Indeed, even the SEC admits that "there is a range of judgments that an issuer might make as to what is 'reasonable' in implementing Section 404 and the Commission's rules." As a result, determination of whether a particular firm has complied with its SOX obligations is highly fact-specific and contextual. In addition, in securities litigation cases, such as those brought under Sarbanes-Oxley, courts have stated that issues of reasonableness and materiality are issues properly left for determination at trial by the jury. Accordingly, the company and its management cannot be certain that they've fully complied with Section 404 until the SEC or a court decides that they've done so. It therefore seems doubtful whether the new guidance will actually result in significant cost savings.

The Run-Up to SOX: The Big Picture

Because Sarbanes-Oxley is a response to a specific set of perceived problems in corporate governance and practice, the act's historical context is essential to understanding the law and complying with its various mandates. After all, as the saying goes, "those who do not learn from history are doomed to repeat it."

As mentioned earlier, the first years of this decade—2000 to 2002—were not happy times on Wall Street. On top of the late 1990s stock market bubble bursting, there also came a string of other bad news that deeply shook investor confidence.

We all know the litany, of course: repeated accounting scandals, of which Enron and WorldCom were merely the most notorious; a high-profile investigation by New York's attorney general calling into question the integrity of stock market analysts; routine restatement of earnings by many blue-chip corporations; allegations of excessive executive compensation; the Martha Stewart insider-trading case; and so on.

Much of the blame was laid at the door of corporate managers and directors. For example, the New York Stock Exchange opined that during the early years of this century we observed a "'meltdown' of significant companies due to failures of diligence, ethics and controls" on the part of directors and senior managers. At Enron, perhaps the most notorious example, an internal investigation concluded that senior managers "were enriched, in the aggregate, by tens of millions of dollars they should never have received." The report further concluded that Enron's "Board of Directors failed . . . in its oversight duties" with "serious consequences for Enron, its employees, and its shareholders."

None of this should have come as a surprise. History teaches that market bubbles are fertile ground for fraud. Cheats abounded during the Dutch tulip-bulb mania of the 1630s. The South Sea Company, which was at the center of the English stock market bubble in the early 1700s, was a pyramid scheme. Fraud was rampant before the Great Crash of 1929. Hence, it was hardly a shock to find fraudsters and cheats when we started turning over the rocks in the rubble left behind when the stock market bubble burst in 2000.

Corporate scandals are always good news for big-government types. After every bubble bursts, going all the way back to the South Sea bubble, new laws always are enacted. Why? Because there is nothing a politician or regulator wants more than to persuade angry investors that he or she is being aggressive in rooting out corporate fraud.

Hence, it was entirely predictable that the shenanigans at Enron, WorldCom, et al., coming after several years of steady decline in the stock market, would lead to regulation. Like a cook who throws spaghetti at the wall to see if it's done, legislators and regulators threw a lot of new rules at corporations to see what stuck: Sarbanes-Oxley, numerous SEC regulations, and California's onerous corporate disclosure act.

Enron: Where It All Began

In many ways, Enron epitomized the rampant financial follies of the late 1990s. Granted, Enron was no Silicon Valley start-up with just a dot-com address. To the contrary, Enron's roots went back to the 1930 formation of the Northern Natural Gas Company. By the early 1990s, following many mergers and name changes, Enron was a large and seemingly highly successful electricity and natural gas distributor with large investments in power plants, pipelines, and other energy utility infrastructure.

For much of the 1990s, the new financial giant looked like a roaring success. It was named one of America's most innovative companies and best employers. In fact, however, there were serious problems behind the façade.

Enron financed its rapid growth and expansion in the 1990s mainly by borrowing. By the late 1990s, Enron was deeply in debt but remained dependent on continued borrowing for expansion and debt service. As the debt mounted, it began to pose a significant threat to Enron's credit rating. In turn, because Enron's energy-trading business was dependent on the company maintaining an investment-grade rating for its debt securities, top Enron management began looking for creative new ways of raising money.

The solution Enron CFO Andrew Fastow hit upon was the use of so-called special purpose entities (SPE), typically limited liability companies or partnerships, which entered into complex transactions with Enron. Although the SPEs technically were independent companies, Enron in fact controlled them and used the money they raised to finance Enron's business ventures.

At the risk of oversimplifying, the basic structure of these deals involved the creation of a limited partnership to which Enron sold stock (or other assets). Using the stock as collateral, the SPE would go to a bank or other lender and borrow money to finance some business venture. Because the SPE had no debts and Enron stock was appreciating so rapidly in value, banks would lend to these SPEs on very favorable terms.

The trick was that under arcane accounting rules, as long as someone other than Enron owned at least 3 percent of the SPE's equity, Enron's consolidated financial statements did not have to disclose the SPE's assets and debts. Hence, these SPE investments were "off balance sheet." By thus concentrating debt in these off-balance-sheet SPEs, Enron hoped that both its credit rating and stock price would remain high despite its increasingly precarious financial situation. So long as investors and analysts remained in the dark, the game could go on.

The SPEs weren't just part of an accounting game, however. Despite the obvious conflict of interest inherent in related-party transactions between a corporation and one of its officers or directors, Enron's board routinely waived its ethics rules to allow Fastow's participation in the SPE deals as a part owner of the SPE. According to a subsequent internal investigation, Fastow made over $30 million in profit from these deals. Several other Enron executives also participated in these deals and likewise made millions. In most of these transactions, Enron's internal controls proved inadequate, not least because Enron managers did not even bother to follow the accounting controls the firm had established.

It all started to unravel when investigative journalists and the SEC finally began taking a serious look at the minutiae of Enron's finances. On October 16, 2001, Enron announced that it was taking a $544 million after-tax charge against earnings and reducing shareholders' equity by $1.2 billion in connection with transactions with just one of Fastow's SPEs. A few weeks later, Enron announced a major restatement of its earnings for the four years 1997–2000 to account properly for transactions with two other SPEs. The restatement devastated Enron's earnings: It reduced Enron's 1997 earnings by $28 million out of $105 million total, 1998 earnings by $133 million out of $703 million, 1999 earnings by $248 million out of $893 million, and 2000 earnings by $99 million out of $979 million. The restatement also increased the amount of debt on Enron's balance sheet by $711 million in 1997, by $561 million in 1998, by $685 million in 1999, and by $628 million in 2000. As a result, Enron slashed shareholder equity by $258 million in 1997, $391 million in 1998, $710 million in 1999, and $754 million in 2000.

Enron's stock price collapsed, dropping from over $90 per share to less than $1. Shareholders and creditors filed numerous lawsuits. Criminal and civil fraud investigations ensued. In December 2001, Enron declared bankruptcy.

In 2004, CFO Fastow copped a guilty plea under which he agreed to testify against former Enron CEO Jeffrey Skilling and chairman Kenneth Lay. Under the deal, Fastow was sentenced to a ten-year prison term. Former Enron executives Michael Kopper and Ben Glisan struck similar deals.

In 2006, Lay and Skilling were convicted of numerous counts of securities fraud and conspiracy. Lay passed away in July 2006. In October 2006, Skilling was sentenced to twenty-four years in prison.

The Other Shoes Drop

The Enron scandal produced a flurry of activity in Congress. Numerous reform bills were introduced. Most of these were mere publicity stunts, however, and meaningful legislative action seemed highly unlikely. But then the other shoes began to drop.

In January 2002, telecommunications giant Global Crossing filed bankruptcy. It soon came out that the company had been misrepresenting its financial situation and manipulating its recognition of revenues. A few months later, the SEC announced an investigation of accounting fraud at WorldCom. It turned out that WorldCom management had inflated the company's assets by over $11 billion, capitalized expenses that should have been incorporated into the earnings statement, and reported phony revenues. WorldCom's own internal audit process uncovered the fraud, which it reported to the company's new outside auditor (KPMG), which notified the board of directors. In this case, unlike Enron, the company's internal controls thus eventually worked, a point that likely strongly influenced Congress's focus on such controls in drafting SOX.

By the time the Global Crossing and WorldCom scandals had wrenched the attention of Congress back to corporate governance, the problem looked to be widespread. The SEC's Division of Enforcement, for example, announced that in the first two months of 2002 alone it brought an unprecedented number of new financial reporting cases (almost triple the number of the comparable period in the prior year, which itself had been a record). In addition, unlike most prior periods, in which the SEC had focused mainly on small fry, the cases brought in 2001–2002 involved a record number of *Fortune* 500 companies.

Although they differed in their details, the scandals at Enron, Global Crossing, WorldCom, and most of the other companies investigated by the SEC during this period all involved some form of accounting fraud. This commonality was underlined by the unfortunate coincidence that Enron, Global Crossing, and WorldCom had used the same accounting firm as their outside auditor; namely, Arthur Andersen. Indeed, Arthur Andersen's name figured prominently in many other cases of accounting fraud in the 1990s and early 2000s, including the scandals at Sunbeam, Waste Management, Qwest, and the Baptist Foundation of Arizona.

By mid-2002, the accounting firm had been indicted, subjected to SEC civil actions, and sued by many companies and their shareholders. In 2002, Arthur Andersen was convicted of obstruction of justice charges arising out of destruction of Enron documents. Although the U.S. Supreme Court later overturned the conviction on technical grounds relating to the jury instructions, the verdict sounded Arthur Andersen's death knell. The storied accounting firm effectively became defunct, with all of its clients and virtually all of its employees gone.

The Failure of the Gatekeepers

Auditing firms such as Arthur Andersen function as gatekeepers—that is, reputational intermediaries between investors and their corporate clients who vouch for those clients. The typical corporation relies on numerous such gatekeepers: auditors, rating agencies, securities analysts, investment bankers, and lawyers. Although the corporate client generally pays these service providers, investors trust information from such providers because the gatekeepers put their own reputations at stake. Because the value of a gatekeeper's services depends on its reputation, the market believes that a gatekeeper is not willing to risk its accumulated goodwill for a single client.

In the 1990s, however, the incentives for gatekeepers to police corporate conduct substantially weakened. Accounting firms typically provided a whole host of services to companies whose books they audited, such as tax preparation and software consulting. Because these other lines of business were more profitable than auditing, the accountants feared to anger management by vigorously pushing audits and challenging management's aggressive accounting treatments.

During that decade, a number of legal changes also reduced gatekeeper liability risk. The Supreme Court's 1994 *Central Bank of Denver* decision, for example, eliminated aiding and abetting liability in private securities fraud cases. The 1995 Private Securities Litigation Reform Act imposed significant restrictions on private securities fraud litigation. The 1998 Securities Litigation Uniform Standards Act abolished state court securities fraud class actions. Columbia securities law professor John Coffee (in an article in *Boston University Law Review*) argues these changes "greatly reduced the incentives of plaintiffs in securities class actions to sue secondary participants such as auditors, analysts, and attorneys," which in turn reduced the incentive for auditors to protect investor interests.

Accountants were not the only gatekeepers who fell down on the job, of course. As we shall see, corporate boards of directors and lawyers also all too often failed to do their jobs. Sarbanes-Oxley and related reforms targeted all of these gatekeepers. Given the centrality of accounting fraud and auditor failures to the pre-SOX story, however, it is not surprising that accounting firms were SOX's principal target. Ironically, we'll see later how accountants have also been SOX's principal beneficiaries.

The Root of All Evil

Enron, Global Crossing, and WorldCom were not isolated cases. Between 2000 and 2002, hundreds of companies restated earnings to adjust for prior flawed accounting practices. Allegations of improper revenue recognition, failure to properly recognize expenses, and cooking the books in a host of other ways were brought against numerous companies. But why did so many managers go bad during this period? In short, greed.

In a burst of financial populism, President Bill Clinton and Congress in 1994 changed the tax laws to cap at $1 million the deduction corporations may take for executive compensation. Performance or incentive-based forms of compensation, most notably stock options, however, were exempt from this cap (as they still are). The result was a dramatic shift in executive compensation away from cash and toward stock options. The stock market bubble of the late 1990s didn't help matters, as constantly rising stock prices made stock options seem like a sure thing.

Compensatory stock options normally issue with a strike price equal to the company's stock market price on the options' issue date. If the company's stock price subsequently rises, the executive can exercise the options and sell the shares at the higher market price. In theory, the resulting potential for profit aligns shareholder and manager interests and thus incents executives to maximize the company's stock price. Both the executive and the corporation may also realize various tax benefits. Here's an example:

> On June 1, 2005, Acme Corporation issues to me options on 1,000 shares with a strike price equal to the then-prevailing market price of $10 per share. One year later, the stock price has risen to $15 per share. I exercise the option, paying Acme $10,000 (the $10 strike price times the 1000 shares I'm buying). I then sell the shares at the market price of $15 per share, for a total of $15,000, realizing a profit of $5,000.

In practice, however, stock options put tremendous pressure on managers to keep the stock price headed up no matter how the company actually was doing. CEOs insisted that the company beat—or, at least, make—the "number" (that is, the consensus forecast by analysts of the company's quarterly earnings). A company that failed to do so could see its stock price fall drastically as analysts complained and investors jumped off the bandwagon, with resulting catastrophic consequences for the value of the firm's executives' stock options. Under this compulsion to make the number, the temptation to resort to accounting trickery proved too much for many managers to bear.

SOX to the Rescue

By mid-2002, then-SEC chairman Harvey Pitt declared that restoring investor "confidence is the No. 1 goal on our agenda." As a first step, the SEC ordered over 900 of the country's largest corporations to certify under oath the accuracy and completeness of their corporate disclosures. This requirement triggered a new wave of high-profile earnings restatements. With the 2002 elections looming, pressure thus grew within Congress for legislative action.

In a remarkably brief period, with minimal legislative processing, Congress slapped together a number of reform proposals that had been kicking around Washington for a long time and sent the mix to President Bush for signing. As Yale law professor Roberta Romano explains in a *Yale Law Review* article:

> Simply put, the corporate governance provisions were not a focus of careful deliberation by Congress. SOX was emergency legislation, enacted under conditions of limited legislative debate, during a media frenzy involving several high-profile corporate fraud and insolvency cases. These occurred in conjunction with an economic downturn, what appeared to be a free-falling stock market, and a looming election campaign in which corporate scandals would be an issue. The healthy ventilation of issues that occurs in the usual give-and-take negotiations over competing policy positions, which works to improve the quality of decision-making, did not occur in the case of SOX.

It's hardly surprising that legislation crafted in such a haphazard fashion turned out to be far more costly than anyone expected. As a business manager or director reading this book, your task is to minimize those costs while still complying with the mishmash of mandates created by SOX.

SOX in Its Legal Context

SOX is not a freestanding statute. Instead, it built upon the existing framework of state corporation codes and federal securities laws that have long governed corporate governance. Accordingly, a quick review of the pre-SOX legal landscape provides the necessary context for understanding the changes worked by SOX.

The Corporation and State Law

A leading legal dictionary defines the corporation as "an artificial person or legal entity created by or under the authority of the laws of a state or nation." Although technically correct, this definition is not especially enlightening. You may find it more helpful to think of the corporation as a legal fiction characterized by six attributes: formal creation as prescribed by state law, legal personality, separation of ownership and control, freely alienable ownership interests, indefinite duration, and limited liability. Taken together, these six attributes—all grounded in state corporation codes—give the corporate form considerable advantages for large businesses as compared to the other forms of business organizations available under U.S. law.

STATE CORPORATION LAW: DELAWARE'S DOMINANCE

Delaware is to corporate law as Michael Jordan is to basketball—the undisputed all-time champ.

The extent to which Delaware dominates the incorporation market is really quite astonishing. Fully 60 percent of *Fortune* 500 companies are incorporated in Delaware. As a result, when Delaware speaks, corporate lawyers and business people listen. Its corporation statute and the cases decided by its courts are the single most important source of corporate law in this country.

Formalities of Creation. Someone creates a corporation by drafting articles of incorporation that comply with the statutory requirements of the state of incorporation. The articles are the most important of the corporation's organic documents. The articles set out the corporation's essential rules of the road—the basic terms under which it will operate. Each state's corporate statute sets forth the minimum provisions the articles must contain. Model Business Corporation Act § 2.02, for example, requires the articles to include the corporation's name, the number of shares the corporation is authorized to issue, the name and address of the corporation's registered agent, and the name and address of the incorporator. In addition, the comments to § 2.02 list numerous other provisions that must be included in the articles if the corporation wishes to avail itself of certain statutory options. Among the more important of these options are provisions relating to division of shares into classes and series and liability of directors.

The incorporator then files the articles with the appropriate state agency, which in most states is the Secretary of State's office. In some states, the Secretary of State's office then issues a document called the certificate of incorporation. In other states, the Secretary of State will simply return a copy of the articles of incorporation along with a receipt to the incorporator. At this point, the corporation has come into existence. The initial board of directors thereupon holds an organizational meeting at which corporate bylaws are adopted, officers are appointed, and other loose ends are tied up.

The bylaws adopted at that meeting are the corporation's chief set of internal operating rules. Other than certain issues that must be addressed in the articles of incorporation, such as the number and types of shares of stock the company is authorized to issue, the bylaws govern most of the corporation's internal affairs. Indeed, the bylaws can address virtually anything one desires. Model Business Corporation Act § 2.06, for example, allows the bylaws to "contain any provision for managing the business and regulating the affairs of the corporation that is not inconsistent with law or the articles of incorporation."

Separation of Ownership and Control. Corporations differ from most other forms of business organizations in that ownership of the firm is formally separated from its control. Although shareholders nominally "own" the corporation, they have essentially no decision-making powers, other than the right to elect the firm's directors and to vote on certain very significant corporate actions. Instead, the statute vests management of the firm in the hands of the board of directors, who in turn delegate the day-to-day running of the firm to its officers, who in turn delegate some responsibilities to the company's employees.

Legal Personality. As a legal matter, the corporation is an entity wholly separate from the people who own it and work for it. For most purposes, the law treats a corporation as though it were a legal person, having most of the rights and obligations of real people, and having an identity wholly apart from its constituents. Corporate law statutes, for example, typically give a corporation "the same powers as an individual to do all things necessary or convenient to carry out its business and affairs."

Perpetual Duration. A corporation is said to have perpetual duration. A more accurate statement, however, is that the corporation has an indefinite legal existence that can be terminated only in rare circumstances. Among these are liquidation in bankruptcy, a vote of the shareholders to dissolve the company, an involuntary dissolution suit, or a merger or consolidation with another corporation.

Free Transferability of Shares. One of the great advantages of the corporate form is that shares of stock are freely transferable. Absent special contractual restrictions, shareholders are free to sell their stock to anybody at any price. A transfer of stock has no effect on the corporation, except that there is now a new voter of those shares. For public corporations, the secondary trading markets greatly facilitate this process.

MANAGERS AND OTHERS

The corporation's senior employees are referred to as its managers (known collectively as the corporation's management). Officers are the most senior managers. A corporation's officers typically include its president (or chief executive officer), one or more vice presidents, a treasurer or chief financial officer, and a secretary.

Contractual exceptions to the rule of free transferability are often found in close corporations, which is one of the many ways in which such firms resemble partnerships more than other corporations. Although shares of stock in a closely held corporation are freely transferable in theory, the lack of a readily available secondary trading market for such shares means they seldom are easily transferable in practice. Moreover, investors in a closely held corporation often prefer to restrict transferability. Like any other personal relationship, the success or failure of a small business often depends upon maintaining a rather delicate balance between the owners. Free transferability of ownership interests threatens that balance. In closely held corporations, shareholders therefore often agree to special contractual restrictions on the alienability of shares.

Limited Liability. The limited liability doctrine holds that shareholders of a corporation are not personally liable for corporate obligations and thus put at risk only the amount of money that they invested in buying their shares. Suppose, for example, that an employee of Acme Co. commits a tort against Paula Plaintiff. Under the tort and agency law doctrine of vicarious liability, Acme is held liable to Plaintiff for $10 million in damages resulting from the employee's tortious conduct. Acme has only $1 million in assets. The limited liability rule bars Plaintiff from seeking to recover the unsatisfied $9 million remainder of her claim from Acme's shareholders. The shareholders' investment in Acme stock may be worthless if Acme becomes bankrupt as a result of Plaintiff's lawsuit, but the shareholders will have lost only that portion of their wealth they invested in Acme.

In rare circumstances, courts may invoke an equitable exception to the limited liability rule called "piercing the corporate veil." If invoked, the veil-piercing remedy allows creditors to hold shareholders personally liable for the corporation's obligations. In the immediately preceding example, if Paula Plaintiff successfully invokes the veil-piercing doctrine, the court will allow her to recover the unsatisfied portion of her claim from Acme's shareholders.

AUTHORIZED SHARES DEFINED

All states require that the articles of incorporation specify the number and classes of shares the corporation is authorized to issue. A corporation may not sell more shares of a class than the number of authorized shares. If the board of directors wishes to issue a greater number of shares than the articles authorize, it must ask the shareholders to amend the articles to increase the number of authorized shares.

For the definition of a number of other key corporate law and governance terms, see the Glossary on page 251.

The Federal Securities Laws

The two federal statutes of principal importance for our purposes are the Securities Act of 1933 and the Securities Exchange Act of 1934. Both statutes share two principal goals: assuring adequate disclosure of material information to investors and preventing fraud.

The 1933 act is principally concerned with the sales of securities by issuers in the primary market—that is, sales by a corporation of its stock or debt securities to investors. It therefore follows a transactional approach to disclosure model: The act focuses on getting information about the specific transaction in question from the issuer to investors.

Because a firm must make the disclosures required by the act every time it publicly sells securities, but need not make the disclosures at other times, the information made available to investors pursuant to its transactional disclosure regime quickly would go stale. Accordingly, the Securities Exchange Act created a companion system of periodic disclosures under which so-called reporting companies are required to provide disclosure to the market on an ongoing basis.

Stock Exchange Listing Requirements

Listing of a company's equity securities for trading on a prestigious stock market, such as the NYSE or NASDAQ, confers significant benefits on the company and its management. The greater liquidity of listed securities relative to those sold in the over-the counter (OTC) market reduces listed issuers' cost of capital. Listing also confers considerable prestige on the firm and its managers. Listed companies therefore desire to remain so, while many unlisted firms pursue eligibility for listing as their primary goal.

Corporate governance thus is regulated not only by the corporation law code of their state of incorporation and the federal securities laws, but also by the contract they sign with the stock exchange on which they have their principal listing. For New York Stock Exchange-listed companies, the NYSE's Listed Company Manual governs. For NASDAQ-listed companies, the Listing Qualifications set out the relevant rules.

READ THE TEXT

The NYSE Listed Company Manual is available online at *www.nyse.com/lcm/lcm_section.html*. NASDAQ's Listing Qualifications are available at *www.nasdaq.com/about/ LegalComplianceFAQs.stm*.

After the Enron scandal broke, the NYSE appointed a blue-ribbon panel of the usual suspects to ride to the rescue. In turn, as a *Wall Street Journal* editorial put it, the panel "anointed boards of directors, especially 'independent directors' as the capitalist cavalry." Specifically, the panel made five major sets of recommendations:

- Enlarging the role and power of independent members of listed companies' boards of directors
- Requiring listed companies to adopt codes of business conduct and corporate governance guidelines
- Requiring shareholder approval of all equity-based compensation plans
- Requiring the CEOs of listed companies to certify annually that the company is complying with NYSE listing standards and that information provided to investors is accurate
- Encouraging the SEC and other regulatory bodies to address accounting, auditing, and disclosure standards

The NYSE board has adopted all of these recommendations. Similar changes were made to the NASDAQ Listing Qualifications. Because these stock exchange listing requirements overlap with SOX in many respects, we'll expand our discussion of SOX and the related SEC rules to include the exchange rules where appropriate.

Enter SOX: Highlights of the New Mandates

Why did the regulatory scheme created by state corporation law, federal securities regulation, and stock exchange listing requirements fail to prevent Enron et al.? As we've seen, the corporate scandals of 2000–2002 arose out of the confluence of two major trends: (1) the incentives to cheat provided by stock option–based compensation and (2) the all-too-frequent inadequacy of existing internal controls and the audit process to detect and prevent cheating. In response, Congress intended for SOX to increase the penalties for securities fraud by corporate executives, require more effective systems of internal control, and improve the audit process. Although we'll examine SOX's key operative provisions in detail in the chapters that follow, a brief overview of the most important provisions will help put things in context.

New Disclosure Rules

Although SOX is mainly a process statute, it does mandate a number of new disclosures. Explicit disclosure is required of off-balance-sheet and related-party transactions, for example. Pro forma earnings statements must be presented in a way that is not misleading and be reconciled with an accompanying presentation prepared in compliance with generally accepted accounting principles (GAAP). Insider stock transactions now must be disclosed within two business days rather than at the end of each month. In the annual report, management must acknowledge its responsibility for maintaining an effective system of internal controls and must provide a written assessment of those controls.

Many of the new disclosure rules are of the therapeutic variety. For example, SOX requires companies to disclose whether they have adopted a code of ethics for their senior financial managers and, if not, why not. Likewise, SOX requires companies to disclose whether the audit committee of their board of directors includes at least one financial expert and, if not, why not. Congress doubtless didn't care about the content of these disclosures. Instead, Congress expected companies would adopt the requisite code of ethics and appoint the requisite financial expert rather than having to offer investors a presumably embarrassing explanation for their recalcitrance.

Auditing, Accounting, and Internal Controls

As noted, while SOX added some new disclosures to those required of public corporations, Congress was concerned principally with the process by which disclosures are prepared and the information within them is gathered and verified. Much of the act thus is concerned with accounting and auditing.

Prior to SOX, the accounting profession was largely self-regulating. Although the 1934 act gave the SEC authority to impose financial accounting standards, the SEC had never done so. Instead, it allowed private sector organizations—especially the Financial Accounting Standards Board (FASB) and the American Institute of Certified Public Accountants (AICPA)—to take the lead in developing the standards by which corporate audits are conducted (known as Generally Accepted Auditing Standards, or GAAS) and the way in which financial statements are presented (GAAP).

Although FASB continues to play an important role under SEC oversight in developing accounting standards, SOX created the Public Company Accounting Oversight Board (PCAOB) as an independent oversight body for the accounting profession. As a result, the AICPA's role in developing auditing standards is now limited to those governing closely held corporations. The SEC is encouraging the PCAOB, FASB, and AICPA to cooperate in ensuring consistent rules for both types of corporations.

The PCAOB has an enormously broad congressional mandate to create accounting rules and to enforce them. It is funded by a general power of de facto taxation over all publicly held companies. There are early indications that the PCAOB's independence and ability to raise its own revenue through taxation is supporting a dramatic expansion in its size and scope. Its 2004 budget was $103 million, and its staff started the year at 126 employees and ended the year with 262 employees. The PCAOB's 2005 budget was another 30 percent higher, at $136 million, and it expected to end that year with 450 employees.

Not everything was left in the PCAOB's lap, however. Instead, Congress took a number of specific actions directed at accounting and auditors. As we saw in our review of the business failures of 2000–2002, for example, a key concern motivating SOX's drafters was the conflicts of interest inherent when accounting firms sell other services to the corporations whose books they audit. Title II of the act therefore limited the extent to which accountants may provide consulting services to their audit clients.

In order to make the outside auditor more independent of corporate managers, SOX's drafters codified the long-standing stock exchange requirement that the board of directors of public corporations must have an audit committee. This board committee must consist entirely of outside directors who meet specified independence standards (we'll look at this requirement in much more detail in Chapter 5). Toward the same end, Congress also made it a crime for company managers to attempt to mislead or coerce an outside auditor.

CEO and CFO Rules

Title III of SOX requires the corporation's CEO and CFO to certify that the company's SEC disclosure documents are free of material misrepresentations or omissions and that the financial statements therein fairly and accurately reflect the company's financial and business condition. Title IX imposes stiff criminal penalties for failing to comply with the certification requirements and even stiffer ones for willfully filing a false certification. In effect, the statute gives the CEO and CFO primary responsibility for the establishment, design, and maintenance of the corporation's internal financial controls. If a corporation is obliged to restate its financial statements due to misconduct, the CEO and CFO must return to the corporation any bonus, incentive, or equity-based compensation they received during the twelve months following the original issuance of the restated financials, along with any profits they realized from the sale of corporate stock during that period. The act prohibits a corporation from directly or indirectly making or even arranging for loans to its directors and executive officers, subject to some minor exceptions. Finally, the act prohibits executives from trading during so-called blackout periods in which the employees participating in 401(k) and other stock-based pension plans are forbidden from trading. If the executive does so, the corporation may sue to recover any profits. If the corporation fails to do so, a shareholder may bring a derivative action akin to those traditionally available to enforce the short-swing profit provision under § 16(b).

New Legal Ethics Rules

When one runs down the now all too familiar list of corporate governance scandals of the new century—Enron, WorldCom, Tyco, ImClone, and Adelphia, to name but a few—one encounters a distressing number of instances in which negligence by corporate lawyers allowed management misconduct to go undetected. Worse yet, lawyers sometimes even acted as facilitators and enablers of management impropriety.

During the Senate floor debate on SOX, Senator John Edwards (D-NC) proposed a last-minute amendment to the bill, which added § 307 and commanded the SEC to develop new legal ethics rules for lawyers appearing before it. In January 2003, the SEC responded by promulgating new rules, the principal substantive feature of which is a so-called up-the-ladder reporting requirement. This requirement creates an early warning system about management wrongdoing through mandatory attorney disclosures to the board of directors.

When a lawyer who appears and practices before the SEC becomes aware of evidence of a material violation by the issuer or by any officer, director, employee, or agent of the issuer, the lawyer's initial duty under the new rules is to report such evidence to the issuer's chief legal or executive officer. Unless the lawyer reasonably believes that that officer has provided an appropriate response within a reasonable time, the lawyer shall report the evidence of a material violation to the audit committee of the board of directors (subject to several exceptions and alternatives).

The SEC thus tried to give lawyers a very simple obligation: You report the violation. If the officers don't properly resolve the violation, you go to the board. As we'll see in Chapter 4, however, it's not that simple.

SOX's Scope

Most of SOX's key operative provisions apply only to reporting companies, that is, corporations required to register with the SEC, or, in colloquial terms, public corporations. Out of the 4 million-plus corporations in the United States, SOX therefore directly affects only about 13,000-odd corporations. Of course, those corporations account for the lion's share of the United States' economic output.

Two of SOX's provisions—those relating to document destruction and protection of whistle blowers—apply not only to reporting companies, but also closely held businesses and nonprofit entities. In addition, many nonprofits and small businesses comply voluntarily with many SOX provisions.

Reporting Companies

Among the reporting companies subject to SOX, so-called "nonaccelerated filers"—that is, companies with a float of less than $75 million—were initially exempted from compliance with SOX § 404's internal control requirements, which are SOX's most costly provisions with which to comply. In August 2006, the SEC announced a proposal for bringing those firms within SOX. Under that proposal, nonaccelerated filers would have to begin providing the management report required by § 404 assessing the effectiveness of the company's internal controls over financial reporting in fiscal years ending on or after December 15, 2007. In addition, nonaccelerated filers would have to begin complying with § 404's requirement to provide the external auditor's attestation report on internal controls over financial reporting in their annual reports as of the first annual report for a fiscal year ending on or after December 15, 2008.

Nonreporting Companies

What about nonreporting companies, such as closely held corporations or nonprofit corporations? Only two of Sarbanes-Oxley's provisions apply directly to nonreporting corporations: (1) The protections for whistle blowers and (2) the prohibition of destroying, altering, or falsifying documents so as to prevent their use or discovery in any official proceeding. As to the former, Board Source and Independent Sector, two leading organizations of nonprofits, recommend that:

> written policies vigorously enforced by executive staff and the board send a message that misconduct isn't tolerated. These policies should cover any unethical behavior within the organization—including sexual harassment.
>
> Each organization must develop procedures for handling employee and volunteer complaints, including the establishment of a confidential and anonymous mechanism to encourage employees and volunteers to report any inappropriateness within the entity's financial management. No punishment for reporting problems—including firing, demotion, suspension, harassment, failure to consider the employee for promotion, or any other kind of discrimination—is allowed. Even if the claims are unfounded, the organization may not reprimand the employee. The law does not force the employee to demonstrate misconduct; a reasonable belief or suspicion that a fraud exists is enough to create a protected status for the employee.

As for the prohibition of document destruction, it applies to any closely held or nonprofit corporation that is potentially subject to official federal proceedings, which could range from tax cases to bankruptcy to criminal or civil investigations of violations of the host of federal laws. Accordingly, all closely held and nonprofit corporations should create written-document retention policies and communicate those policies to any administrative personnel who handle the nonprofit's books or records. The policy should specify the period for which documents are retained and procedures for destruction of documents older than the required retention period. Education of personnel handling documents is critical to prevent accidental or innocent destruction in violation of the established policy.

SAMPLE POLICY

A good example of a combination document-preservation and whistle blower protection policy for nonprofits is available from the Council of Michigan Foundations at *www.cmif .org/documents/whistleblower.doc.*

What about Mom-and-Pops?

The universe of closely held for-profit corporations ranges from giants like Cargill (with over $66 billion in revenue and 115,000-plus employees in 2005) down to the proverbial mom-and-pop. Technically, so long as they are nonreporting companies, none of these corporations are obliged to comply with SOX.

Larger close corporations, however, face a number of pressures to "voluntarily" comply with the main SOX provisions: First, larger close corporations often have at least some independent board members, who may see SOX compliance as a way of limiting their liability exposure and enhancing their ability to oversee management. Second, larger close corporations often use one of the Big Four accounting firms for auditing or other services. These firms reportedly are pressuring their nonreporting clients to develop policies for substantially complying with SOX's core provisions. Finally, close corporations considering going public in the near future will be required to be SOX-compliant thereafter and, accordingly, typically begin implementing SOX's mandates even while they are still private.

There is no bright line that divides close corporations that ought to be SOX-compliant from those that need not do so. As a rule of thumb, however, many lawyers and accountants suggest that any company with annual revenues of $50 million or more should seriously consider implementing at least the basic SOX mandates, especially those relating to auditor independence and effective internal controls.

Nonprofit Entities

As with closely held corporations, the other provisions of SOX do not apply directly to nonprofit corporations. However, California has adopted a Nonprofit Integrity Act, which extends a number of SOX-like provisions to nonprofits, most notably:

- Nonprofit corporations with gross revenues of $2 million or more must prepare annual financial statements and have them audited by an independent certified public accountant. These financial statements must be audited in accordance with GAAS and prepared in accordance with GAAP.
- Nonprofit corporations with annual gross revenues of $2 million or more must establish and maintain an audit committee. The audit committee is to be appointed by the nonprofit's board of directors or comparable governing body. The committee may include persons who are not members of the board of directors, but may not include employees or staff members of the nonprofit, the nonprofit's treasurer or CFO, or the nonprofit's president or CEO. Subject to oversight by the board of directors, the audit committee supervises the hiring, firing, and compensation of the nonprofit's independent CPA.

Similar legislation has passed or is under active consideration in a number of other states.

Nonprofits face two other sources of pressure to become SOX-compliant. First, many nonprofit boards of directors include a substantial number of members who are also directors of public corporations. These individuals typically are familiar with SOX compliance and reportedly are pressuring their fellow board members to adopt voluntarily SOX-like policies. Second, nonprofits that have their financial statements audited by independent CPAs report significant pressure from their accountants to adopt SOX-like policies, especially with respect to internal controls and audits. This development isn't particularly surprising. As we'll see in Chapter 7, accountants turned out to be the chief beneficiaries of Sarbanes-Oxley.

In the face of these pressures, many larger nonprofits have opted to become more-or-less SOX-compliant. Indeed, a 2006 study by Foley & Lardner confirms that "nonprofit organizations continue to adopt more aspects of the Sarbanes-Oxley Act than for-profit companies." Overall, nonprofits were more likely to have implemented or planned to implement whistle-blower procedures, board approval of nonaudit services by auditors, and restrictions on executive compensation, among other areas of reform.

2

Disclosure to Investors:
Securities Regulation Before and After SOX

The late Supreme Court justice Louis Brandeis famously opined that: "Sunlight is . . . the best of disinfectants; electric light the most efficient policeman." In passing SOX, Congress intended to shine new light into some previously dark corners of corporate governance and accounting. Specifically, Congress wanted to shake up the relationship between the managers of a corporation and its shareholders by strengthening and expanding the disclosures publicly held corporations are obliged to provide to investors.

SOX's disclosure sections build upon the long-standing disclosure mandates of the federal securities laws and can only be understood when situated in that context. Accordingly, we'll start this chapter with an overview of the pre-SOX federal disclosure scheme and then examine the myriad ways in which SOX tweaked that scheme.

The Federal Securities Laws: An Overview

Regulation of the U.S. securities markets began with the passage of the first state "blue sky law" by Kansas in 1911. Unfortunately, state regulation was largely ineffective: The statutes had a limited jurisdictional reach, they contained many special interest exemptions, and the states had limited enforcement resources.

In the aftermath of the Great Crash of 1929 and subsequent Great Depression, there was general agreement that the time had come for federal regulation of the securities markets. Between 1933 and 1940, Congress passed seven statutes regulating various aspects of the industry. The two key laws for our purposes are the Securities Act of 1933 and the Securities Exchange Act of 1934.

READ THE TEXT

The SEC's Web site offers free copies of the full text of the securities laws and the regulations thereunder. *Go to www .sec.gov/about/laws.shtml.*

Back in 1933, Congress considered three different models of securities regulation that states used in their blue sky laws:

- The merit model: Review by a state official of a proposed offering of securities to determine whether the deal included provisions that were "unfair, unjust, inequitable or oppressive" and whether it offered "a fair return."
- The fraud model: Simply prohibit fraud in the sale of securities, with civil and/or criminal penalties for committing fraud.
- The disclosure model: Allow issuers to sell very risky or even unsound securities, provided they gave buyers enough information to make an informed investment decision.

In adopting the Securities Act of 1933, Congress opted for a mix of the latter two approaches. As a result, there is no merit review of whether investors will earn a decent return or the terms of the deal are fair. In theory, the act allows you to sell investors a rotten egg, as long as you tell them very clearly that the egg is rotten.

The Pre-SOX Disclosure Regime

State corporate law never has had very much to say about disclosure to investors. Instead, it is the federal securities laws that are the source of virtually all corporate disclosure obligations. Indeed, disclosure was the chief vehicle by which the act's drafters intended to regulate the markets.

Transactional and Periodic Disclosure

As originally adopted, the Securities Act and the Securities Exchange Act established two separate disclosure systems. The Securities Act imposes transactional disclosure obligations, requiring disclosure in connection with particular transactions. Most importantly, Securities Act § 5(a) makes it unlawful to sell a security unless a registration statement is in effect with respect to the securities. In other words, unless an exemption is available, the prospective issuer must file a registration statement with the SEC and wait for the registration statement to become effective before selling securities. The registration statement includes the prospectus, which is the disclosure document given investors.

In contrast, the Securities Exchange Act created a system of periodic disclosures for certain companies. This created a certain amount of overlap and duplication. In the early 1980s, the SEC adopted a program of integrated disclosure, which partially combined the two systems. Under the integrated disclosure system, an issuer planning a registered offering follows a three-step procedure. It first looks to the various registration statement forms to determine which form it is eligible to use. The issuer then looks to Regulation S-K for the substantive disclosure requirements. Regulation S-K adopted uniform disclosure standards for both acts, so that virtually all filings are now prepared under identical instructions. As a result, the style and content of disclosure documents under both acts are now essentially identical. Finally, Regulation C provides the procedural rules.

The registration statement forms and Regulation S-K spell out in great detail the information that must be contained in the registration statement. But their requirements do not tell the complete story. The registration statement must not only contain the information specifically required by the forms, but also must contain any additional material information that is necessary to give investors a clear picture of the company and the securities it is offering. The SEC recently required that portions of the prospectus be written in "plain English," a requirement whose utility remains open to debate.

Registered Offering Terminology

In a registered offering, the issuer is the corporation that sold the securities. The underwriter is an investment bank that specializes in selling securities to investors on behalf of their issuers. For a definition of various terms involved in the underwriting of offerings, see the Glossary on page 251.

Because many companies go years or even decades without selling securities to the public, a disclosure regime based solely on transactional disclosures soon would result in the market being dominated by stale information. In order to ensure that public corporations provide information about their finances and business to investors on an ongoing basis, the Securities Exchange Act created the system of periodic disclosure.

Only corporations registered with the SEC must comply with the periodic disclosure rules. This result follows from Securities Exchange Act § 13(a), which requires periodic reports from any company registered with the SEC under § 12 of the act. In turn, § 12(a) requires that any class of securities listed and traded on a national securities exchange (such as the New York or American Stock Exchanges) must be registered with the SEC under the Securities Exchange Act. In addition, § 12(g) and the rules thereunder require all other companies with assets exceeding $10 million and a class of equity securities held by 500 or more record shareholders to register that class of equity securities with the SEC.

SAMPLE FORMS

You can download sample periodic disclosure forms, along with official commentary, from the SEC's Web site at *www.sec.gov/about/forms/secforms.htm#1934forms*.

The periodic reports required by the Securities Exchange Act include: (1) Form 10, the initial Securities Exchange Act registration statement. It is only filed once with respect to a particular class of securities. It closely resembles a Securities

Act registration statement. (2) Form 10-K, an annual report containing full audited financial statements and management's report of the previous year's activities. It usually incorporates the annual report sent to shareholders, but also includes extensive additional disclosures. (3) Form 10-Q, filed for each of the first three quarters of the year. The issuer does not file a Form 10-Q for the last quarter of the year, which is covered by Form 10-K. Form 10-Q contains unaudited financial statements and management's report of material recent developments. (4) Form 8-K, which must be filed within fifteen days after certain important events affecting the corporation's operations or financial condition, such as bankruptcy, sales of significant assets, or a change in control of the company.

The SEC's Web site also makes available a searchable electronic database of all disclosure forms filed with it at: *www.sec .gov/edgar/searchedgar/webusers.htm.*

Post-SOX, the SEC divided the universe of registered corporations into three subcategories: First, *large accelerated filers*, defined as companies with a market float of $700 million or more. Second, *accelerated filers*, defined as companies having a float of at least $75 million, but less than $700 million. Third, *nonaccelerated filers*, defined as companies with a float of less than $75 million.

The first two categories of companies have a reduced amount of time following the end of a fiscal quarter or year to file their quarterly and annual reports. Large accelerated filers must file their annual report within sixty days of the end of the fiscal year and their quarterly reports within forty days of the end of a quarter. Accelerated filers must file their quarterly reports on the same schedule, but have seventy-five days from the end of the fiscal year to file their annual reports. Nonaccelerated filers have ninety days from the end of the fiscal year and forty-five days from the end of the quarter to file the respective reports.

If a corporation is required to register under the Securities Exchange Act, it also becomes subject to the proxy rules under § 14, the tender offer rules under § 13 and § 14, and certain of the act's antifraud provisions.

Reading Financial Statements

At the core of the 10-K and 10-Q reports are the company's financial statements, audited in the case of the former and unaudited in the latter. The two basic financial statements are the balance sheet and the income statement. The difference between these two statements is often analogized to that between a snapshot and a motion picture. The balance sheet provides a snapshot of the corporation's financial structure at a given point in time, while the income statement shows the corporation's profits or losses over a period of time.

FLOAT

A company's outstanding shares constitute its "float." The float can be expressed either as the number of shares outstanding or, more often, as the total market value of the outstanding shares.

Here's a simplified balance sheet for the Acme Corporation at the end of its most recent fiscal year.

Consolidated Balance Sheet of Acme Corporation, as of December 31, 20XX

ASSETS		LIABILITIES (DEBT)	
Current assets		Current liabilities	
Cash	$ 195,000	Accounts payable	$ 15,000
Accounts receivable	$ 75,000	Short-term notes	$ 60,000
Securities	$ 30,000	**Total Current Liabilities**	**$ 75,000**
Total Current Assets	**$ 300,000**		
		Long-term notes payable	$ 325,000
Fixed assets			
Plant and equipment	$ 790,000	**Total Liabilities**	**$ 400,000**
Less depreciation	($ 360,000)		
Land	$ 70,000	Paid-in capital	$ 175,000
Total FixedAssets	**$ 500,000**	Retained earnings	$ 225,000
		Total Shareholder Equity	
Total Assets	**$ 800,000**		**$ 400,000**
		Total Debt and Equity	**$ 800,000**

The balance to which this statement's name refers is between assets on the left side and liabilities and shareholders' equity on the right side. A balance sheet is balanced when a corporation's total assets equal its total liabilities plus shareholders' equity.

The income statement is a report showing the profit or loss from a firm's operations over a given period of time, typically a fiscal year or quarter. It's designed to answer the question: "How profitable is the business?" The figure below shows a simplified sample income statement for Acme Corporation.

Income Statement of Acme Corporation
FY 20XX

Sales revenue		$ 850,000
Cost of goods sold		550,000
Gross profit		$ 300,000
Operating expenses:		
Marketing expenses	$ 90,000	
General and administrative expenses	80,000	
Depreciation	30,000	
Total operating expenses		$ 200,000
Operating income		$ 100,000
Loss on sale of securities		(20,000)
Earnings before taxes		$ 100,000
Income tax (25%)		(25,000)
Net income		$ 75,000

The basic income statement equation is Sales – Expenses = Profits. Key expenses typically include costs of producing the company's products or services, operating expenses (such as marketing, selling, general and administrative expenses, and depreciation), one-time charges, financing costs (interest paid), and taxes.

The principal change made by SOX to the balance sheet and income statement is the requirement discussed below of greater disclosure of off-balance-sheet transactions. In addition, the company must disclose any corrections or adjustments made to the financial statements by the outside auditors. Finally, note that the SEC and plaintiffs' lawyers are closely scrutinizing corporate balance sheets and income statements for the sort of accounting fraud that characterized the Enron era. Improper recognition of revenue, capitalizing expenses, and similar financial statement trickery can result in significant corporate and personal liability.

Many of the terms used in the balance sheet are not only of accounting, but also of legal, importance. If you're not certain of the meaning of any of the most important terms on a balance sheet—*assets* (current and fixed), *accounts receivable, depreciation, goodwill, liabilities* (current and long-term), *shareholder's equity*—you can find definitions of them in the Glossary on page 251.

Civil Liabilities for Securities Fraud

Before the Securities Act's adoption, securities fraud was solely the province of state common law—under which it was treated just like any other kind of fraud. Plaintiff had to prove that the defendant had misrepresented a material fact. Plaintiff also had to prove all of the other elements of common law fraud: reliance, causation, scienter (advance knowledge), and injury. Finally, plaintiff's recovery was limited to the amount of loss: the difference between what he paid and what the securities were truly worth. In light of these limitations, the common law was almost incapable of dealing with securities fraud. Many securities cases, for example, involve omissions—failures to speak. But how does a plaintiff show reliance on silence?

As a result, prior to the federal securities laws, securities fraud cases were rare and even more rarely successful. To achieve its goal of attacking fraud in securities transactions Congress therefore adopted civil and criminal liability provisions far more liberal than those available at common law.

A person who violates the securities laws faces three possible antagonists. First, the SEC. Securities Act § 20(a) gives the SEC broad power to investigate violations of the act or the SEC rules adopted under the act. Section 20(b) gives the SEC

47

the power to bring a civil action in U.S. District Court seeking an injunction against ongoing or future violations. A number of other sanctions are potentially available under other statutes. For example, the SEC can suspend or bar a professional underwriter, broker, or dealer from working in the securities industry. The SEC may also impose a variety of administrative penalties on violators.

Second, the Justice Department. Section 20(b) authorizes the SEC to refer securities violations to the attorney general who may then institute criminal proceedings against the violator.

Finally, the plaintiff's bar. Many plaintiffs' lawyers handle securities cases on an occasional basis. In addition, however, there is a small, but active and very capable, group of plaintiffs' lawyers who specialize in securities litigation under the civil liability provisions discussed below.

Liability for Fraud in Primary Market Transactions

The Securities Act contains two express private causes of action for securities law violations. Section 11 creates an important but limited civil liability for fraudulent registration statements. The chief limitations on § 11 are (1) its restriction to securities sold through the use of a registration statement and (2) its requirement that the actionable misrepresentation or omission appear in the registration statement. Hence, for example, § 11 does not reach fraudulent oral communications or written communications other than the registration statement.

There is an extensive list of possible defendants under § 11(a):

1. Anyone who signed the registration statement. Section 6(a) requires the registration statement to be signed by the issuer, the issuer's principal executive officers, the issuer's

chief financial officer, the issuer's principal accounting officer, and a majority of the issuer's directors.

2. Plaintiff may also sue every director of the issuer at the time the registration statement became effective, every person named in the registration statement as someone about to become a director, every expert named as having prepared or certified any part of the registration statement, and every underwriter involved in the distribution. Most courts hold that this list is exclusive and, consequently, that there is no aiding and abetting liability under § 11.

The issuer is strictly liable under § 11. Other defendants, however, can escape § 11 liability if they prove they used due diligence in preparing and reviewing the registration statement. As a practical matter, due diligence is delegated to lawyers. The issuer's directors and officers rely on the corporation's counsel to conduct a due diligence investigation. The underwriter relies on its counsel to conduct such an investigation. Only experts normally conduct their own due diligence. If the lawyer's conduct satisfies the standards set forth above, the parties who relied on the lawyer get the benefit of the due diligence defense. If not, all parties who relied on the lawyer lose their defense, but may have a malpractice action against the lawyer. This makes conducting a due diligence investigation one of the most nerve-wracking assignments a young corporate lawyer faces.

Section 12(a)(2) is the general civil liability under the Securities Act for fraud and misrepresentation. Although it overlaps somewhat with § 11, § 12(a)(2) is a broader remedy. Liability under § 12(a)(2) arises not only in connection with material misrepresentations or omissions in a registration statement, but also in connection with misrepresentations or omissions made in other writings or oral statements used in connection with any public offering.

Section 12(a)(2) imposes private civil liability on any person who offers or sells a security in interstate commerce, who makes material misrepresentation or omission in connection with the offer or sale, and cannot prove he or she did not know of the misrepresentation or omission and could not have known even with the exercise of reasonable care. Plaintiff's prima facie case thus has six elements: (1) the sale of a security; (2) through instruments of interstate commerce or the mails; (3) by means of a prospectus or oral communication; (4) containing an untrue statement or omission of a material fact; (5) by a defendant who offered or sold the security; and (6) that defendant knew or should have known of the untrue statement (if plaintiff pleads defendant's knowledge, the burden of proving otherwise shifts to the defendant). Notice that plaintiff need not prove reliance.

A key issue in § 12(a)(2) litigation is the question of who is a seller. This is significant because the class of permissible defendants under § 12(a) is narrower than under any of the other major antifraud provisions: Only sellers can be held liable. The Supreme Court has held that persons in contractual privity with the plaintiff (that is, persons with a legally recognized interest in the matter) are sellers for purposes of § 12(a). In addition, the Court held that someone not in contractual privity with the plaintiff may still be deemed a seller if he "successfully solicits the purchase, motivated at least in part by a desire to serve his own financial interests or those of the securities owner." Brokers or other agents who assist the issuer in soliciting sales thus face liability. On the other hand, the privity requirement sharply limits the scope of secondary liability, so that participants in the offering who do not engage in soliciting or selling activities—such as accountants and lawyers—generally cannot be held liable.

Securities Exchange Act § 10(b) and Rule 10b-5

Rule 10b-5 is easily the most famous, and arguably the most important, of all the SEC's many rules:

It shall be unlawful for any person, directly or indirectly, by the use of any means or instrumentality of interstate commerce, or of the mails or of any facility of any national securities exchange,

(a) To employ any device, scheme, or artifice to defraud,

(b) To make any untrue statement of a material fact or to omit to state a material fact necessary in order to make the statements made, in the light of the circumstances under which they were made, not misleading, or

(c) To engage in any act, practice, or course of business which operates or would operate as a fraud or deceit upon any person, in connection with the purchase or sale of any security.

On its face, the rule does not tell us very much other than that fraud in connection with securities transactions is a bad thing. The central theme of the rule's history thus is one of repeated judicial glosses on the relatively innocuous text. As former chief justice William Rehnquist once observed, Rule 10b-5 is "a judicial oak which has grown from little more than a legislative acorn."

Rule 10b-5 applies to both affirmative misrepresentations and passive omissions. Two aspects of Rule 10b-5, as applied to omission cases, are especially important. First, not all omissions give rise to liability. Instead, liability can be imposed only if the defendant had a duty to speak.

Second, reliance and transaction causation are presumed in omission cases. In private party litigation under Rule 10b-5, plaintiffs generally must prove that they reasonably relied upon the defendant's fraudulent words or conduct. Plaintiffs also must prove both transaction causation and loss causation. The former is analogous to "but for" causation in tort law—it is a showing that defendant's words or conduct caused plaintiff to engage in the transaction in question. Loss causation is somewhat analogous to the tort law concept of proximate causation—it involves showing that the defendant's words or conduct caused plaintiff's economic loss. In omission cases, both transaction causation and reliance generally are presumed so long as plaintiffs can show defendant had a duty to disclose and failed to do so.

Under Rule 10b-5, only material misrepresentations or omissions are actionable. Materiality is determined by asking whether there is a substantial likelihood that a reasonable investor would consider the information important in deciding how to act.

One can easily mislead investors without intending to do so. Even an honest mistake might cause some to be misled.

As such, it is not apparent that liability for securities fraud should be premised on intent. Tort law encourages drivers to drive more safely, because they can be held liable for negligent accidents. Tort law also encourages manufacturers to put out safer products by imposing strict liability for defective products. Should securities law be any less rigorous in encouraging accurate disclosure?

Liability in fact can be imposed for unintentional misrepresentations under some securities law provisions. Sections 11 and 12(a)(2) of the 1933 Securities Act, for example, require no evidence from plaintiff with respect to the defendant's state of mind. Instead, state of mind is at most an affirmative defense under these provisions. In order to make out the state-of-mind—that is, due diligence—defense, moreover, defendants must show that they were nonnegligent.

Under Rule 10b-5, however, the Supreme Court has held that plaintiff's prima facie case must include proof defendant acted with scienter, which the court defined as a mental state embracing intent to deceive, manipulate, or defraud. Although this formulation clearly precludes Rule 10b-5 liability for those who are merely negligent, the Supreme Court left open the issue of whether recklessness alone met the scienter requirement. Subsequent lower-court decisions have generally held that recklessness suffices.

Post-SOX Disclosure Obligations

Although SOX is concerned mainly with processes, especially the outside audit and internal controls, and governance, especially the role of directors, it does impose a number of new disclosure requirements; these will be discussed in the next few sections of this chapter. Most are intended to provide investors with more and better information about their portfolio companies, but some are more in the nature of corporate therapy designed to change management behavior.

Because Enron's collapse was such a central motivator behind SOX's ultimate adoption, and because failure adequately to disclose its off-balance-sheet transactions was so critical to Enron's problems, it comes as no surprise that one of Congress's first orders of business was to mandate better and more complete disclosure of such transactions. More precisely, in SOX § 401, Congress told the SEC to adopt "rules providing that each annual and quarterly financial report . . . shall disclose all material off-balance sheet transactions, arrangements, obligations (including contingent obligations), and other relationships of the issuer with unconsolidated entities or other persons, that may have a material current or future effect on financial condition, changes in financial condition, results of operations, liquidity, capital expenditures, capital resources, or significant components of revenues or expenses."

In 2003, the SEC responded by issuing a new rule requiring reporting companies to create a separately captioned subsection of the "Management's Discussion and Analysis" (MD&A) section of their annual and quarterly reports providing a detailed explanation of any off-balance-sheet arrangements.

For purposes of this rule, "off-balance-sheet arrangements" include:

- Certain guarantee contracts, such as standby letters of credit; stock price guarantees; guarantees that scheduled contractual cash flows from individual financial assets will be collected; performance guarantees; and agreements to indemnify based on changes relating to assets, liabilities, or equity securities of the indemnified party. These are precisely the sort of undisclosed guarantees Enron gave creditors of its SPEs.

- Retained or contingent interests in assets transferred to a SPE that are not included in the company's consolidated financial statements.
- Derivative instruments classified as equity.
- Material variable interests in unconsolidated SPEs held by and material to the issuer if the unconsolidated SPE provides financing, liquidity, market risk, or credit risk support to, or engages in leasing, hedging, or research and development services with, the issuer.

Arrangements captured by any of these definitions must be disclosed if they have, or are reasonably likely to have, a present or future material impact on the registrant's financial condition, changes in financial condition, revenues or expenses, results of operations, liquidity, capital expenditures, or capital resources. An off-balance-sheet transaction will be deemed material where it is substantially likely that the reasonable investor would consider it important.

When disclosure of an off-balance-sheet transaction is required, management must provide in narrative form information about the nature and business purpose of the transaction, the significance of the transaction with respect to the reporting company's liquidity and capital resources, the transaction's financial impact on the company, and the extent to which it changes the company's exposure to risk. The company must also identify for investors known events, demands, commitments, trends, or uncertainties that may affect the company's ability to benefit from the off-balance-sheet transaction.

In order to prevent the requirement from degenerating into routine boilerplate and to ensure full disclosure, the SEC requires that the MD&A discussion include not only the information specified in the rule but also any other information necessary for an understanding of the off-balance-sheet transaction and its effect on the company.

Enhanced MD&A Disclosure

The SEC long ago decided that the raw numbers provided by a reporting company's financial statements were not enough to give investors a full picture. The MD&A therefore provides narrative overview of management's assessment of results of the previous year's operations. In addition, management increasingly includes forward-looking information such as forecasts, future goals, and upcoming projects. While the MD&A is not audited, the information is very useful to analysts and investors.

Although SOX did not mandate changes in MD&A disclosure, the SEC chose the MD&A section as the vehicle for more complete disclosure of off-balance-sheet transactions. At about the same time (mid-2003), the SEC also announced new guidance for preparing the rest of the MD&A section. In doing so, the SEC made clear its dissatisfaction with how many companies were preparing their MD&A and, in particular, what the SEC believed was an increasing use of boilerplate language. The SEC therefore designed the 2003 guidance "to elicit more informative and transparent MD&A that satisfies the principal objectives of MD&A: (1) to provide a narrative explanation of a company's financial statements that enables investors to see the company through the eyes of management; (2) to enhance the overall financial disclosure and provide the context within which financial information should be analyzed; and (3) to provide information about the quality of, and potential variability of, a company's earnings and cash flow, so that investors can ascertain the likelihood that past performance is indicative of future performance." In addition, the SEC encouraged companies to involve their top management in reviewing MD&A disclosures instead of leaving it to their lawyers. Corporate CEOs and CFOs need to be particularly conscious of this suggestion. Indeed, in their case it is really more of a mandate, because the MD&A section is one of the pieces of information in annual or quarterly reports that SOX requires CEOs and CFOs to certify "fairly presents, in all material respects, the financial condition and results of operations of the issuer." Hence, there is a significant new source of potential liability for CEOs and CFOs if the MD&A disclosures are incomplete or misleading in any material respect.

For New York Stock Exchange–listed companies, not only top management but also the audit committee of the board of directors must be actively engaged with the preparation of the MD&A disclosures. Section 303A.07 of the NYSE Listed Company Manual requires that the audit committee review and discuss the company's annual audited financial statements and quarterly financial statements with both management and the independent auditor. The provision makes specific reference to the committee's duty to review the company's MD&A disclosures. In a guide published by the Practicing Law Institute, attorney Ottilie Jarmel recommends that:

> To discharge these duties effectively, the audit committee needs to be involved periodically throughout the process and be given plenty of lead time. Its review should culminate in a comprehensive walk-through of the MD&A and the financial statements and footnotes, . . . highlighting changes from the prior year and reasons for the change, whether due to a business development, new disclosure requirement, or new accounting pronouncements.

The 2003 guidance laid particular emphasis on the following areas: First, large companies with extended MD&A sections should begin their disclosure with an executive summary to provide an overview of the information to come. Second, companies should determine what information is most important and give it the most prominent mention. Third, companies should identify and discuss those key performance indicators, including nonfinancial performance indicators, that their own managers use to assess the company's performance. Relevant indicators might include such items as plant capacity and utilization data, inventory backlogs, employee turnover rates, sales data, interest rates charged the company, and customer satisfaction metrics. Fourth, companies must provide some forward-looking information by identifying and disclosing those trends, events, demands, commitments, and uncertainties that are known to management and reasonably likely to have a material effect on the company's financial condition or operating results. In this area, the SEC has been particularly focusing on the need for disclosures about trends that might affect liquidity. Finally, the commission emphasized that "MD&A should not be merely a restatement of financial statement information in a narrative form," but rather should provide an analysis by management of how the company is really doing and its immediate prospects.

In a 2004 speech at Northwestern University Law School, SEC commissioner Cynthia Glassman explained that: "Management should give investors information about the quality and potential variability of the company's earnings and cash flow, so investors can assess whether past performance is indicative of future performance." She also advised lawyers to "work with management to give a detailed analysis of important year-to-year changes and trends that are material to operations" and to advise their "clients to spend more time talking about liquidity, cash flow and capital resources."

This new SEC emphasis is illustrated by a lawsuit the commission filed against two former top Kmart executives for misleading investors about Kmart's financial condition in the months preceding the company's bankruptcy. According to the commission's complaint, former CEO Charles Conaway and former CFO John McDonald were responsible for material misrepresentations and omissions about matters relating to the company's liquidity in the MD&A of Kmart's Form 10-Q for the quarter ended October 31, 2001. Specifically, the MD&A section allegedly "failed to disclose the reasons for a massive inventory overbuy in the summer of 2001 and the impact it had on the company's liquidity." The MD&A disclosure made by Kmart under the executive's auspices attributed the inventory changes to "seasonal inventory fluctuations and actions taken to improve our overall in-stock position," but the SEC claimed much of the inventory buildup resulted from a reckless purchase of $850 million of excess inventory. The SEC further alleged that the defendants dealt with Kmart's liquidity problems by slowing down payments owed vendors to the tune of some $570 million by the end of the quarter in question. The MD&A section thus allegedly failed to disclose the impact of Kmart's liquidity problems on the company's relationship with its vendors. It also failed to disclose the fact that many vendors stopped selling to Kmart during the fall of 2001.

Another good example is the SEC enforcement proceeding against former executives of Global Crossing. Global Crossing announced pro forma earnings results that were consistently higher than those calculated according to GAAP. The SEC took the position that failure to disclose the reasons for the discrepancies in the MD&A section of Global Crossing's filings constituted an omission of material facts.

If you suspect that MD&A disclosures have gotten longer as a result of this new guidance and tougher enforcement posture, you're right. Indeed, this is just part of a major post-SOX problem: investor information overload. In theory, greater disclosure enables shareholders to make decisions that are more informed. Basic economics, however, tells us that a rational investor will expend the effort to make an informed decision only if the expected benefits of doing so outweigh its costs. Given the length and complexity of SEC disclosure documents, the opportunity cost entailed in becoming informed before voting is quite high and very apparent. Moreover, most shareholders' holdings are too small to have any significant effect on corporate policy or effectiveness.

READ THE TEXT

You can download the entire text of the SEC's 2003 guidance from its Web site at *www.sec.gov/rules/interp/33-8350.htm*.

If shareholders are rationally apathetic, information that is more comprehensible thus will not lead to better decisions. To the contrary, greater volumes of information will only make the situation worse.

The SEC knows that this is a problem. Indeed, the 2003 guidance expressly states that a company "should avoid the unnecessary information overload for investors that can result from disclosure of information that is not required, is immaterial, and does not promote understanding" of the company's "financial condition, liquidity and capital resources, changes in financial condition and results of operations (both in the context of profit and loss and cash flows)."

The trouble with this advice is that the securities laws define materiality by asking whether there is a substantial likelihood that the reasonable investor would consider the information to be important in deciding how to act. This is the sort of standard lawyers love and business people hate, because it's almost impossible to provide clear guidance ex ante. In close cases, you can't know for sure whether information was material or not until a jury tells you so (and you've exhausted all appeals). Accordingly, in light of the enormous liability consequences for failing to disclose material information, most lawyers counsel their clients to err on the side of disclosure.

Reporting GAAP Versus Pro Forma Earnings

In order to ensure uniformity in how companies present their financial data, corporate financial statements are required to be prepared in accordance with GAAP. Hence, a corporation's outside auditor will only provide an unqualified opinion certifying the company's financial statements if those statements are fully compliant with GAAP. These accounting industry-wide principles traditionally derived from a number of sources, including FASB rules and AICPA guidance. Increasingly, however, they will be set or, at least, influenced by the PCAOB.

Corporations have long complained that GAAP requires them to disclose too many unusual and nonrecurring financial events—a cynic might note that the complaints center on unusual expenses rather than income—and thus present a misleading financial picture to investors. In the 1990s, it became common for companies to issue earnings reports on a so-called pro forma basis, which excluded allegedly unique and/or nonrecurring transactions. Because the excluded items were almost always expenses, pro forma earnings typically were higher than earnings calculated pursuant to GAAP, often significantly.

The practice of pro forma reporting is problematic for two reasons. First, because there are no rules to define what transactions are excluded, there is no uniformity to pro forma accounting. As a result, it is almost impossible to compare one corporation to another. Second, many of the corporate decisions about what to exclude in calculating pro forma results were highly suspect. As a result, pro forma accounting often proved even more misleading for investors than did GAAP-compliant disclosures.

In SOX, Congress did not ban pro forma reporting of earnings, as some proposed. Instead, companies that use pro forma accounting in earnings statements must also disclose GAAP-compliant results, giving the latter at least equal prominence.

Therapeutic Disclosures

As we saw in Chapter 1, Congress and the SEC have sometimes used disclosure rules to effect substantive changes in corporate conduct. In such cases, the regulators don't really care what the corporation says about Topic X, they want the corporation to do something about Topic X. SOX contains several requirements of this type.

Management must include in its annual and quarterly reports a statement acknowledging its responsibility for creating and maintaining adequate systems of internal controls. Management also must provide a narrative assessment of the effectiveness of those controls. In addition, the company's outside auditor must evaluate and attest to management's assessment. Because these disclosures are so closely tied into the substantive requirements relating to internal controls, we'll defer detailed consideration of them until Chapter 7.

SOX § 406 requires reporting companies to disclose whether they have adopted a code of ethics for the company's top financial managers and, if not, why not. In order for the company to claim it has adopted the requisite code of ethics, the code must establish standards "reasonably necessary to deter wrongdoing and to promote honest and ethical conduct, including the ethical handling of actual or apparent conflicts of interest between personal and professional relationships." The code must provide for avoidance of conflicts of interest, by identifying an appropriate person to whom the covered officers must disclose any material transaction or relationship that reasonably could give rise to a conflict between the officer's personal interest and business duties. The code must obligate the officers covered to ensure "full, fair, accurate, timely, and understandable disclosure" in reports and documents filed by the company with the SEC. The code must mandate personal and corporate compliance with applicable governmental laws, rules, and regulations. It should provide for prompt internal reporting of code violations to an appropriate person or persons, whom the code should identify. The code should be filed with the SEC as an exhibit to the company's annual report and posted to the company's Web site. Obviously, Congress figured that few companies would dare go to the shareholders and say, "we're not going to have a code of ethics." In any case, because the code of ethics is part and parcel of the CFO's relationship with the corporation, we'll defer further detailed discussion of it until Chapter 3.

SOX § 506 similarly requires the corporation to disclose whether or not its audit committee includes at least one financial expert. We'll look at this requirement in Chapter 6 in connection with our review of the many new rules affecting the audit committee.

Federal Versus State Regulation

Why didn't Congress just order companies to adopt the code and appoint the expert? The likeliest explanation is some continuing respect for federalism.

While there has been a long-standing debate over whether Congress, as a matter of sound policy, should adopt federal corporate governance standards, no one seriously doubts its ability to do so under the Commerce Clause of the U.S. Constitution. To date, however, Congress has chosen not to do so. Instead, Congress has left substantive regulation of corporate governance to state law. Even the vast expansion of the federal role begun by the New Deal securities regulation laws left the internal affairs and governance of corporations to the states.

For over seven decades, corporations thus have been subject to a dual regulatory regime. It is state law, for example, that determines the rights of shareholders. State law thus determines such questions as which matters the board of directors acting alone may authorize and which the shareholders must authorize. State law typically requires, for example, that certain control transactions, such as mergers or sales of substantially all corporate assets, be approved in advance by the shareholders and establishes the vote required (often a supermajority) for shareholder approval of such matters. State law likewise regulates the conduct of shareholder meetings, specifies who may call such meetings, and prescribes whether, and the procedures by which, actions may be taken without a shareholder meeting.

State law also governs most of the rights and duties of corporate directors. As the U.S. Supreme Court once explained, "the first place one must look to determine the powers of corporate directors is in the relevant State's corporation law. 'Corporations are creatures of state law' and it is state law which is the font of corporate directors' powers." State law defines the directors' powers over the corporation, for example. State law establishes the vote required to elect directors. State law determines whether shareholders have the right to cumulative voting in the election of directors, whether the corporation's directors may have staggered terms of office, and whether shareholders have the right to remove directors prior to the expiration of their term of office.

In contrast, federal law traditionally has been concerned mainly with disclosure obligations, as well as procedural and antifraud rules designed to make disclosure more effective. The collapse of Enron and WorldCom, however, along with the varying degrees of fraud uncovered at too many other companies, reinvigorated the debate over state regulation of corporate governance. Many politicians and pundits called for federal regulation not just of securities but also of internal corporate governance, claiming it would restore investor confidence in the securities markets.

In drafting SOX, Congress declined to override expressly the traditional dividing line between state regulation of the substance of corporate governance and federal regulation of disclosure. In several cases, however, Congress used therapeutic disclosure to provide a very modest fig leaf for creeping federalization of certain aspects of corporate governance. As we'll see in Chapter 5, the NYSE's and NASDAQ's new listing requirements regulating director independence are another example of the creeping process of federalization. Taken together, SOX and the new listing requirements constitute the most dramatic expansion of federal regulatory power over corporate governance since the New Deal.

The Need for More and Faster Form 8-K Disclosures

In the stock market, a fiscal quarter is the equivalent of a geologic era. Much of the information disclosed in a quarterly or annual report will be stale within days of the report's release. Accordingly, the SEC's periodic disclosure system long has included Form 8-K as a vehicle for intraquarterly disclosure of significant events. Traditionally, only really major events— such as a merger or acquisition, a change of corporate name or domicile, bankruptcy, or appointment of a different auditor— required disclosure on Form 8-K. As the SEC has observed, however, technological changes make it possible for companies to collect and analyze information far more quickly than was the case when the periodic disclosure regime was created:

> Technological developments that significantly reduce timeframes for the capture and analysis of information necessitate a new consideration of the timing of mandated disclosure to the markets. We believe it would enable investors to make investment and voting decisions on a more timely and better informed basis, provide more timely information regarding management's view of company performance or prospects, protect investors, and promote fair dealing in company equity securities if companies were required to report additional information related to these subjects on a more current basis.

In light of these developments, SOX § 409 directed that reporting companies must "disclose to the public on a rapid and current basis . . . information concerning material changes in the financial condition or operations of the issuer, in plain English, which may include trend and qualitative information and graphic presentations." Congress left it to the SEC to decide how to implement that mandate, which the SEC chose to do through expanding the Form 8-K disclosure obligation.

Under SEC rules adopted in 2004, a Form 8-K must be filed no later than four business days after the occurrence of any of the specified triggering events. (Under the old rules, the filing deadline was either five business days or fifteen calendar days, depending on the nature of the triggering event.) The events triggering the disclosure obligation, and the relevant information that must be disclosed on Form 8-K, include:

1. The entry into, amendment of, or termination of a "material definitive agreement" that was "not made in the ordinary course of business." The date on which the contract was signed, amended, or ended and a description of its key terms must be provided. Employment contracts and compensation plans for top directors and officers generally are considered material contracts, as are agreements for the acquisition or disposition of significant amounts of assets outside the scope of ordinary business.

2. When a company enters into bankruptcy or a receivership.

3. The acquisition or disposition of "a significant amount of assets, otherwise than in the ordinary course of business." This triggering event will often work to supplement the requirement for disclosure of a material agreement.

4. New material financial obligations must be disclosed, with a summary of the key terms. Similar disclosure

is required if the company becomes directly or contingently liable for a material obligation arising out of an off-balance-sheet arrangement. For either purpose, a material obligation would include a capital lease, an operating lease, a long-term debt, or a short-term debt that arises other than in the ordinary course of business. Whether a debt is long or short term for this purpose depends on its duration. Anything over one year is deemed long term.

5. Any event that accelerates or increases the company's obligations under any of the agreements specified in point 4. Obviously, for example, defaulting on a covered debt obligation must be disclosed.

6. Exit from or cessation of a business activity must be disclosed if "material charges will be incurred under generally accepted accounting principles applicable to the company."

7. The company must disclose "a material charge for impairment to one or more of its assets, including, without limitation, an impairment of securities or goodwill," when such a charge "is required under generally accepted accounting principles applicable to the company."

8. If the company is delisted from its stock exchange, transfers its listing to another exchange, or fails to comply with stock exchange listing requirements, disclosure is required.

9. Sales of the company's equity securities that were not registered with the SEC under the 1933 Act. For most issuers, sales need not be disclosed if the aggregate amount sold is less than 1 percent of the outstanding shares.

10. Material modifications of the rights of security holders, such as amendments to the articles of incorporation

that change the rights of stockholders or amendments to bond indentures.

11. A change in the company's outside auditor. The reasons for the change should also be given.

12. A restatement of earnings or other financial statements.

13. A number of changes at the top must be disclosed, including a change in the controlling shareholder (if any), departure of directors or officers, election of directors, and appointment of principal officers (such as the CEO or CFO).

14. Any amendments to the articles of incorporation or bylaws must be announced on Form 8-K.

Taken together, these changes represent a dramatic increase in the amount of real-time disclosure companies are obliged to make. Given the very short filing deadline, companies must put into place dependable processes for promptly channeling information about triggering events to a central clearinghouse charged with preparing and filing Form 8-K disclosures. To be sure, the SEC adopted a safe harbor assuring companies that they will not lose their eligibility to use a short-form Securities Act registration statement or incur securities fraud liability solely because of a failure to timely file a Form 8-K, provided that the information that should have been disclosed on Form 8-K is reported in the next quarterly or annual report. Not all triggering events are covered by the safe harbor, however; specifically, disclosures relating to changes in the outside auditor or delisting from the principal stock exchange are not covered in this assurance. In addition, the safe harbor does not preclude the SEC from imposing other penalties on those who fail timely to file. (Note that the safe harbor only insulates reporting companies from liability for failure to timely file a Form

8-K; material misrepresentations or omissions of material fact in a Form 8-K remain actionable.)

A best practices approach to handling the new Form 8-K disclosure requirements would include setting up a central clearinghouse that will be responsible for preparing and filing Form 8-Ks. If the company has a permanent disclosure committee, that committee is likely the best agency to deal with the Form 8-K disclosures. If the company does not have a disclosure committee, it should consider establishing one, as creation of such a committee appears to be rapidly becoming a best practice. If formed, the committee likely should include the principal accounting officer (or controller), the chief legal officer (aka, general counsel) or any other senior legal staffer tasked with responsibility for disclosure, the director of risk management, the chief investor relations officer, and the chief media relations officer. Heads of business units particularly likely to generate SEC disclosure obligations are also good candidates for committee membership. In addition to acting as a central clearinghouse, the disclosure committee should prepare a written disclosure policy and train key employees to comply with the policy.

Next, the company should identify those employees who have authority to execute material definitive agreements or take other actions that would trigger the need to file a Form 8-K. These individuals should be educated and trained to identify a triggering event and to provide the clearinghouse with the necessary disclosures. In order to minimize the company's exposure to the risk of failing to file, the company might usefully consider limiting the number of people who have authority to act on the company's behalf in connection with triggering events to the smallest possible number.

The processes used to prepare required disclosures for quarterly and annual reports should be expanded to include looking for any undisclosed events that should have resulted in the filing of a Form 8-K. Ensuring that any such events are disclosed in the next quarterly or annual report, so as to avail oneself of the safe harbor, is essential to minimizing liability exposure. Note that these processes are part of the package of internal control items as to which the company must provide certifications.

Investor and media relations departments should be trained to forward all news releases or other public announcements to the central clearinghouse for evaluation of whether a Form 8-K triggering event has occurred. This is especially important because some Form 8-K disclosure obligations are triggered by a public announcement of the event.

Enhanced SEC Scrutiny

Pre-Enron and its ilk, the SEC frequently failed to audit proactively corporate disclosures. In many cases, the disclosures effectively went from the mailroom to a filing cabinet with little or no SEC staff review.

It's hard to blame the SEC for allowing this situation to develop. The SEC has limited resources, so it must make staffing priority decisions. In addition, SEC staffers rarely have much more information about companies than is available from the face of the disclosure documents. As such, disclosure review didn't seem cost-effective.

Congress, however, concluded that the lack of proactive SEC oversight was an important contributing factor to the scandals at Enron, WorldCom, and their fellow miscreants. Accordingly, SOX § 408 mandates that the SEC conduct a review of every reporting company's disclosure filings at least once every three years. In addition, Congress provided funding for the SEC to increase significantly staffing of the Division of Corporation

Finance, which is the SEC branch principally responsible for conducting the mandated reviews.

The SEC intends to review filings by larger public corporations at least once a year, which is a reverse of prior policies that implicitly assumed fraud was mainly a problem in smaller companies. As we saw in Chapter 1, post-Enron, the SEC realized that *Fortune* 500 companies were at least as likely to have serious disclosure issues as small firms. In addition, in deciding which companies to review and how often to do so, the SEC considers such factors as whether there have been any recent material financial restatements, whether the company's stock price has shown significant volatility, the company's market capitalization, any price/earnings disparities for the company's stock relative to peers, and whether the company conducts operations that are significant to any material sector of the U.S. economy.

SEC review under § 408 is unlikely to entail any sort of on-site audit, at least in the absence of major problems coming to light. Instead, SEC review likely will consist of SEC staffers comparing the document under review with other disclosure documents filed by the company with the SEC, conducting Internet and electronic database searches for information relevant to the disclosures required in the form under review, reviewing the company's own Web site, and the like. In the event the staff discovers problems or questions, it likely will ask the company to furnish written responses to questions or provide supplemental materials. After the review is completed, the SEC staff likely will ask the issuer to correct any identified material deficiencies and/or to make changes in how it prepares such disclosures in the future. Note that effective August 1, 2004, all such staff comment letters and company replies are made available to the public via the SEC's Web site and third-party databases such as LexisNexis or Westlaw.

3

New Duties and Liabilities for Corporate Management

In a famous 1919 case, *Dodge v. Ford Motor Co.,* a group of Ford Motor Company shareholders filed a lawsuit challenging the way Henry Ford was running the company. Specifically, they claimed that Ford had cut the company's dividend so as to reduce prices for the benefit of customers and raise wages for the benefit of employees. At trial, Ford testified that he thought the company had "made too much money," that the company's profits should be shared with its various stakeholders, and that the shareholders should be content to take what he gave them. In a frequently quoted passage, the Michigan Supreme Court rebuffed Ford, stating that:

> A business corporation is organized and carried on primarily for the profit of the stockholders. The powers of the directors are to be employed for that end. The discretion of directors is to be exercised in the choice of means to attain that end, and does not extend to a change in the end itself, to the reduction of profits, or to the nondistribution of profits among stockholders in order to devote them to other purposes.

Today, corporate directors and officers generally recognize their duties to their shareholders. A 1995 National Association of

Corporate Directors (NACD) report, for example, stated: "The primary objective of the corporation is to conduct business activities with a view to enhancing corporate profit and shareholder gain," albeit subject to the qualification that "long-term shareholder gain" may require "fair treatment" of nonshareholder constituents. A 1996 NACD report on director professionalism set out the same objective, without any qualifying language on nonshareholder constituencies. A 1999 Conference Board survey found that directors of U.S. corporations generally define their role as running the company for the benefit of its shareholders. The 2000 edition of Korn/Ferry International's well-known director survey found that when making corporate decisions directors consider shareholder interests most frequently, albeit also finding that a substantial number of directors feel some responsibility toward stakeholders.

Corporation law and governance provide a number of carrots and sticks designed to ensure director and officer fidelity to shareholder interests: in particular, changes in director and executive compensation. For example, it is becoming common to compensate both directors and officers in stock rather than cash and to establish minimum stock ownership requirements as a qualification for election. Tying up a proportion of directors' and officers' personal wealth in stock of the corporation supposedly helps align the directors' and officers' interests with those of shareholders.

As we saw in Chapter 1, however, the existing system of carrots and sticks proved inadequate to deter self-aggrandizing conduct by some executives. Some of those who worked at—and wrecked—firms like Enron or WorldCom doubtless were simply bad apples. Others, however, appear to have been basically decent people who succumbed to temptation. Indeed, in many cases, they seem to have convinced themselves they were doing the right thing. After all, there is nothing quite so easy to rationalize as that which is in one's own self-interest.

STAKEHOLDERS DO MATTER

As suggested by the aphorism "a rising tide lifts all boats," shareholders' long-run interests often are well served by decisions (such as charitable giving or employee-friendly work policies) that appear likely to hurt the bottom line in the short-run. It's perfectly appropriate in both law and practice for boards of directors and managers to look for win-win scenarios, which make all of the business's stakeholders better off. At the bare minimum, as the American Bar Association's Corporate Director's Guidebook explains, boards and managers may conduct the firm's business "with due appreciation of public expectations, taking into consideration relevant legal, public policy, and ethical standards."

Much of Sarbanes-Oxley therefore aims straight at top corporate managers and directors. Congress added a host of new sticks with which it hoped to deter future Enrons. In this chapter, we look at those specifically targeting managers and other corporate employees. In Chapter 5, we'll look at those targeting directors.

CEO and CFO Certifications

Part of the SEC's initial reaction to the Enron scandal was an order requiring the CEOs and CFOs of 947 large corporations to file written certifications that their company's latest annual report and any subsequent disclosure documents were free of material misrepresentations or omissions. Congress liked this idea so much that it incorporated it into SOX—twice.

SOX § 302 provides that when a reporting corporation files either an annual or quarterly report both the CEO and CFO must individually certify that he or she has reviewed the report and, to his or her knowledge, the report does not contain any material misrepresentation or omission of material fact. Both officers must also certify that, to their knowledge, the financial statements and other financial information contained in the report fairly present in all material respects the corporation's financial condition and results of operations for the period covered by the report.

This half of § 302 was—and remains—pretty much of a yawner. As law professor Lawrence Cunningham observes in a *Connecticut Law Review* article:

> [T]his sort of certification requirement—that the statements comply with regulations and fairly present results—has always been a requirement of the federal securities laws. Those singled out to make the certifications, CEOs and CFOs, are invariably named as defendants in private securities lawsuits and SEC enforcement actions. . . . The most this provision did was shine attention on the subject, not an incidental effect but far more modest than was widely believed.

At best, he further observes, this half of § 302 simply heightened corporate "executive attention to the stakes" in play when their companies make disclosures.

It is the second half of § 302 that made a significant change in corporate practice. Specifically, this part of § 302 was designed to give CEOs and CFOs a potent stake in the internal controls processes we'll be reviewing in Chapter 5. It thus requires both the CEO and CFO individually to acknowledge in writing that they are responsible for establishing and maintaining the corporation's systems of internal controls and to certify that such internal controls are designed to ensure that material information properly flows from the corporation's business units to the CEO and CFO. They also must certify that they have evaluated the effectiveness of those internal controls within the ninety-day period prior to the filing of the report. To ensure that the certification is not mere boilerplate, the CEO and CFO are required to include in the quarterly or annual report, as the case may be, an assessment of the effectiveness of the company's internal controls.

Section 302 also requires that the CEO and CFO individually certify in writing that they have disclosed to the outside auditors and the audit committee "all significant deficiencies in the design or operation of internal controls which could adversely affect the issuer's ability to record, process, summarize, and report financial data and have identified for the issuer's auditors any material weaknesses in internal controls." They must also certify to having told the auditors and audit committee about "any fraud, whether or not material, that involves management or other employees who have a significant role in the issuer's internal controls." Finally, they must identify any significant changes in internal controls subsequent to the date of their evaluation, including any actions taken to correct any significant deficiencies and material weaknesses in those controls.

As Cunningham explains:

These provisions look to prevent CEOs and CFOs from hiding behind the defense of ignorance. The clear line of provenance points to the Enron scandal, amid which several senior executives testified before Congress that they lacked knowledge of underlying financial fraud, contending that they couldn't possibly be aware of all activities, including fraudulent practices, within the massive company.

Now, however, we run into an oddity. As noted above, Congress liked the certification idea so much that they put it into SOX in two different places. In addition to the various certification requirements of § 302, § 906 amended the federal criminal code to add a new provision requiring that each "periodic report" filed with the SEC be accompanied by a written certification from the CEO and CFO that the "periodic report . . . fully complies with" the relevant statutes and that the "information contained in the periodic report fairly presents, in all material respects, the financial condition and results of operations of the issuer."

This § 906 certification requirement does not expressly cross-reference the certification mandated by § 302, which raises all sorts of difficult questions. Does a certification made pursuant to the more detailed requirements of § 302 satisfy the obligation under § 906? Does a false § 302 certification expose one to the criminal penalties under § 906? While § 302 clearly applies only to 10-Q and 10-K reports, does § 906 apply not only to them but also to other periodic disclosures (such as Forms 8-K) that contain financial statements? Can a CEO or CFO qualify his or her certification under § 906 by stating that "to my knowledge" the report complies? Unfortunately, we have very little clear guidance on any of these subjects.

Best Practices for CEO and CFO Certifications

Per Regulation S-K Item 601, the § 906 certification should be filed as an exhibit to the annual or quarterly report, as the case may be. The SEC has stated that the company may either file (1) a single § 906 certification signed by both the CEO and CFO or (2) two separate certifications signed by the CEO and CFO individually. The figure below provides a sample form of certification. Note that it includes, in brackets, an optional "to our knowledge" qualifier. Because criminal liability under § 906 requires proof of knowledge, the qualifier is probably unnecessary, but conservative counsel likely would urge its inclusion on the same theory that prompts some folks to wear both a belt and suspenders.

SERIOUS PENALTIES

Just in case you were thinking that the amending of the federal criminal code by § 906 of SOX is not a serious matter, the penalty portion of § 906 is given here, with no comment necessary.

"(c) CRIMINAL PENALTIES.—Whoever—

"(1) certifies any statement as set forth in subsections (a) and (b) of this section knowing that the periodic report accompanying the statement does not comport with all the requirements set forth in this section shall be fined not more than $1,000,000 or imprisoned not more than 10 years, or both; or

"(2) willfully certifies any statement as set forth in subsections (a) and (b) of this section knowing that the periodic report accompanying the statement does not comport with all the requirements set forth in this section shall be fined not more than $5,000,000, or imprisoned not more than 20 years, or both."

Sample Form of Certification Pursuant to Section 906

In connection with the [Quarterly or Annual] Report of [insert corporation's full legal name] (the "Company") on Form [10-Q or 10-K] for the period ending _____ as filed with the Securities and Exchange Commission on the date hereof (the "Report"), we, [insert CEO's name], Chief Executive Officer of the Company, and [insert CFO's name], Chief Financial Officer of the Company, certify, pursuant to 18 U.S.C. § 1350, as adopted pursuant to § 906 of the Sarbanes-Oxley Act of 2002, that [to our knowledge]:

1. The Report fully complies with the requirements of section 13(a) or 15(d) of the Securities Exchange Act of 1934; and
2. The information contained in the Report fairly presents, in all material respects, the financial condition and result of operations of the Company.

This statement shall not be deemed to be "filed" for any purpose whatsoever.

/s/

[insert CEO's full name]
Chief Executive Officer
[insert date]

/s/

[insert CFO's full name]
Chief Financial Officer
[insert date]

The SEC has prescribed a mandatory Form of Certification to be used pursuant to § 302. You must use *exactly* the language set forth in the Form. Separate copies of the Form must be signed by the CEO and CFO and filed as exhibits to the 10-K or 10-Q, as the case may be. The following figure sets out the required text. (Note that a slightly different version is available for use by issuers of asset-backed securities.)

Mandatory Section 302 Form of Certification

I, [identify the certifying individual], certify that:

1. I have reviewed this [specify report] of [identify registrant];

2. Based on my knowledge, this report does not contain any untrue statement of a material fact or omit to state a material fact necessary to make the statements made, in light of the circumstances under which such statements were made, not misleading with respect to the period covered by this report;

3. Based on my knowledge, the financial statements, and other financial information included in this report, fairly present in all material respects the financial condition, results of operations and cash flows of the registrant as of, and for, the periods presented in this report;

4. The registrant's other certifying officer(s) and I are responsible for establishing and maintaining disclosure controls and procedures (as defined in Exchange Act Rules 13a-15(e) and 15d-15(e)) and internal control over financial reporting (as defined in Exchange Act Rules 13a-15(f) and 15d-15(f)) for the registrant and have:

    (a) Designed such disclosure controls and procedures, or caused such disclosure controls and procedures to be designed under our supervision, to ensure that material information relating to the registrant, including its consolidated subsidiaries, is made known to us by others within those entities, particularly during the period in which this report is being prepared;

(b) Designed such internal control over financial reporting, or caused such internal control over financial reporting to be designed under our supervision, to provide reasonable assurance regarding the reliability of financial reporting and the preparation of financial statements for external purposes in accordance with generally accepted accounting principles;

(c) Evaluated the effectiveness of the registrant's disclosure controls and procedures and presented in this report our conclusions about the effectiveness of the disclosure controls and procedures, as of the end of the period covered by this report based on such evaluation; and

(d) Disclosed in this report any change in the registrant's internal control over financial reporting that occurred during the registrant's most recent fiscal quarter (the registrant's fourth fiscal quarter in the case of an annual report) that has materially affected, or is reasonably likely to materially affect, the registrant's internal control over financial reporting; and

5. The registrant's other certifying officer(s) and I have disclosed, based on our most recent evaluation of internal control over financial reporting, to the registrant's auditors and the audit committee of the registrant's board of directors (or persons performing the equivalent functions):

(a) All significant deficiencies and material weaknesses in the design or operation of internal control over financial reporting which are reasonably likely to adversely affect the registrant's ability to record, process, summarize and report financial information; and

(b) Any fraud, whether or not material, that involves management or other employees who have a significant role in the registrant's internal control over financial reporting.

Date: _____

/s/

_____

[name]

[Title]

The CEO and CFO need not replicate the internal or external audit as part of the certification process, but some element of due diligence is necessary. As a matter of best practice, the CEO should receive what might be called "mini-302 certifications" from subordinates providing for their areas of responsibility the affirmations and certifications required by § 302. The certifying officer should meet with the outside auditor to confirm that it has had unrestricted access to conduct its audit and has met with the audit committee. Likewise, the certifying officer should meet with the audit committee to ensure that it has met with the outside auditor and to determine whether the committee knows of any material problems or deficiencies. Finally, the CEO and CFO should meet with the disclosure committee and the head of internal audit to ensure that the information necessary to prepare the corporation's disclosure statements is properly flowing within the firm.

DOES EXECUTIVE CERTIFICATION ADD VALUE?

Economists Utpal Bhattacharya, Peter Groznik, and Bruce Haslem studied the stock price of companies that failed to comply with the SEC's executive certification requirement. They found that those companies experienced no abnormal stock price movements, unusual trading volume, or price volatility. Accordingly, they concluded that requiring CEOs and CFOs to certify the corporation's financial statements was not "value relevant." If they're right, the considerable expense companies incur to comply with the certification requirement has no benefit for shareholders.

You can read their study at *http://papers.ssrn.com/sol3/ papers.cfm?abstract_id=332621.*

Because certification covers the MD&A disclosures, the certifying officers should meet with those responsible for drafting the MD&A. Even if the MD&A is drafted internally, it may be appropriate to have outside counsel review the disclosures.

WHY DID SCRUSHY GET OFF?

In the first criminal trial brought under SOX, former Health-South CEO Richard Scrushy won acquittal on charges of filing false certifications. Executives of other companies should not take too much comfort from that case, however, as Scrushy did so mainly by winning over the jury pool before and during trial. *BusinessWeek* later reported that Scrushy's charitable foundation donated heavily to prominent local African American churches, whose pastors regularly attended the trial and became known as Scrushy's Amen Choir (the jury pool was mainly African American).

Indeed, counsel can be quite helpful throughout this process. Counsel can advise the CEO and CFO on conducting the requisite precertification assessment, memorialize the assessment process in an appropriate diligence report, and assist with identifying areas of particularly high risk. As for the cost, well, let's be honest. If you could buy an insurance policy using somebody else's money, doesn't it make sense to do so? The CEO and CFO are putting their necks on the line here, but the company pays both the general counsel and outside lawyer. The temptation to spend the shareholders' money on legal advice will prove irresistible. If you like, think of it as part of the CEO and CFO's pay package.

Information technology is another way CEOs and CFOs can spend the shareholders' money to satisfy the § 302 certification requirement. Post-SOX, business software companies rapidly ramped up software packages designed to facilitate compliance with the statute's various mandates. A typical § 302 compliance software package will provide for automated management generation of questionnaires to be completed by subordinates, consolidate responses into a single report, flag any material problems, and store documentation in an electronic database. Packages that automate both the § 302 and § 404 compliance processes in a single system have become increasingly common and often are the most cost-effective solution.

CFO Code of Ethics

As a matter of best practice, corporations long have had conflict of interest policies applicable to top management and directors. Such policies are necessary to minimize liability exposure in connection with related party transactions between the corporate entity and one or more of its officers and directors. You'll recall that Enron had just such a policy, but it proved ineffective because the board of directors routinely waived the rules so as to allow Fastow and other Enron executives to invest in the SPEs used to finance Enron's operations.

In SOX, Congress quite specifically targeted Fastow's behavior. (You'll recall the old aphorism that all generals prepare to fight the last war.) SOX § 406 required the SEC to adopt rules pursuant to which a corporation must disclose whether it has adopted a code of ethics for its CFO. The company also must promptly disclose any waivers of that code. As with other examples of therapeutic disclosure incorporated into the act, Congress likely expected that even though this mandate nominally allowed companies to decline to adopt such a code so long as the company disclosed that it had declined and set out its reasons for doing so, few companies would dare risk the public embarrassment, negative media reports, and shareholder complaints likely to follow such a refusal.

In adopting the requisite rule, the SEC took it upon itself to expand the congressional mandate to "require a company to disclose" in its annual report "whether it has adopted a code of ethics that applies to the registrant's principal executive officer, principal financial officer, principal accounting officer or controller, or persons performing similar functions." If the company decided not to adopt such a code, it must explain why it did not do so. If the company does adopt such a code, it must make it publicly available in one of three ways: (1) Post the code to the company Web site (many companies have done so, making corporate Web sites an excellent resource for gathering sample codes); (2) file the code as an exhibit to the annual report; or (3) include in the annual report a statement that a copy of the code will be provided free of charge to anyone who requests a copy.

In order for the company to state that it has adopted a SOX-compliant code of ethics, the SEC rule requires that the code contain "written standards" "reasonably designed to deter wrongdoing" and affirmatively promote:

- Honest and ethical conduct, specifically including handling of related-party transactions and other "actual or apparent" conflicts of interest.
- "Full, fair, accurate, timely, and understandable disclosure" in all public communications and all reports filed with the SEC.
- Compliance by management with laws, rules, and regulations applicable to the company's business.

- Prompt reporting of code violations to an appropriate supervisor or the board of directors.

As a matter of good practice, the company should make copies of the code available to all covered personnel. It also should conduct documented training sessions, so as to satisfy the obligation to promote code compliance proactively.

TAKE A MINUTE

As a matter of good practice, any action by a board of directors with respect to a related-party transaction involving either officers of the company or members of the board should be recorded in the minutes of the board meeting at which the action was taken.

The code should specify who is authorized to grant waivers from compliance with any of the code's terms. Typically, as a matter of best practice, waivers of conflicts of interest on the part of the very senior managers covered by the requisite code should be effected by a committee consisting solely of independent directors. Among other things, approval by such a committee effectively eliminates exposure to liability under the state corporate law fiduciary duty of loyalty as it relates to interested-party transactions. If the corporation has a corporate governance committee consisting of such directors, that would be an appropriate body to evaluate and act on waiver requests. In many corporations, however, responsibility for such corporate governance matters is assigned to the audit, compensation, or nominating committee. In any case, if a waiver is granted, the company must file a Form 8-K disclosing the nature of the waiver, the person or persons to whom the waiver was granted, and the date on which the waiver was made.

Stock Exchange Code Requirements

Both the NYSE and NASDAQ have adopted listing requirements mandating a code of ethics for top management. NASDAQ's Rule 4350(n) piggybacks on SOX § 406 and the SEC rules thereunder by simply requiring listed companies "to adopt a code of conduct complying with the definition of a 'code of ethics'" as established by the SEC. In contrast, NYSE Listed Company Manual § 303A.10 goes considerably further than the SEC version.

With respect to conflicts of interest, for example, the NYSE requires that the code specifically address possible usurpation of business opportunities by managers: "Employees, officers and directors should be prohibited from (a) taking for themselves personally opportunities that are discovered through the use of corporate property, information or position; (b) using corporate property, information, or position for personal gain; and (c) competing with the company." Of course, since state law fiduciary duties already prohibit such conduct, the most this provision does is to highlight the issue and ensure its inclusion in employee policy training.

An NYSE-compliant code of conduct apparently must also establish a baseline for corporate social responsibility. Employees and directors are obliged to "deal fairly with the company's customers, suppliers, competitors and employees." Likewise, the code should "proactively promote compliance with laws, rules and regulations, including insider trading laws."

As a matter of best practice, NYSE-listed companies should adopt a single code of conduct designed to satisfy both the SEC and stock exchange requirements. Because there are no inconsistencies between the two sets of rules, the simplest procedure is to adopt an NYSE-compliant code; as such a code's provisions will be more than adequately expansive to ensure SEC compliance.

Restrictions on Loans to Insiders

SOX § 402 prohibits a corporation from directly or indirectly making or even arranging for loans to its directors and executive officers, subject to some minor exceptions. Granted, loans can be used to hide executive compensation. From a tax perspective, salary and dividends are taxable to the recipient, but the proceeds of a loan are not taxable income. From an accounting perspective, loans are corporate assets, so the money in a sense stays on the books, while the company must deduct salary and dividends from assets.

Yet, it's not at all clear that a flat prohibition—rather than just enhanced disclosure of insider loans—was appropriate. Section 402 directly pre-empts the interested party transaction provisions of state corporate law, which currently permit the making of loans to directors and officers provided the loans are approved by a majority of the disinterested directors or the shareholders. Worse yet, the act fails to define the two key operative terms: "personal loans" and "extensions of credit." Under state corporate law indemnification statutes, for example, corporations frequently do (and in some cases must) advance legal expenses to covered officers and directors. Given the sweeping language of the prohibition on "extensions of credit," some observers believe that the act effectively prohibits any such advancement of funds. In support of such an interpretation, they cite Delaware case law holding that advancement of expenses "is essentially simply a decision to advance credit." In March 2006, however, a federal court held that § 402 does not prevent a corporation from advancing expenses to officers or directors pursuant to state indemnification statutes. Even so, it would be helpful if the SEC were to at least provide guidance on this issue—and, better yet, define those terms by rule.

THE ECONOMICS OF EXECUTIVE LOANS

Yale law professor Roberta Romano has written that "executive loans in a large class of cases served their purpose well, [by] aligning the manager's and shareholders' interest. The blanket prohibition of executive loans in SOX, from this perspective, is self-evidently a public policy error. The provision in the original Senate bill, which was consistent with the conventional federal regulatory approach, required disclosure of executive loans and did not prohibit them. Such an approach would have been far less problematic than the final legislative product from the perspective of shareholder welfare. It would have had the effect of facilitating the termination of loans most unlikely to benefit shareholders, by highlighting their presence to investors who could then place those loans' elimination onto a corporate governance agenda (in the many states where they would otherwise not be involved because shareholder approval of loans is not required). Instead, the legislation is a blunderbuss approach that prohibits all loans, whether or not they are useful in facilitating the shareholders' objective of providing a sought-after incentive effect." You can read her study of SOX at *http://papers.ssrn.com/ sol3/papers.cfm?abstract_id=596101*.

Contrary to conventional wisdom, § 402 does not prohibit all loans to insiders. Exempt transactions include:

- Loans outstanding before SOX was passed
- Corporate credit cards issued to employees
- Borrowing against a 401(k) account
- Margins loans by a brokerage house to its employees
- Loans by financial institutions to their employees

On the other hand, § 402 prohibits not only loans made directly by the corporation to its insiders, but also prohibits the corporation from arranging "for the extension of credit." As a result, an employer can no longer arrange for a bank to lend money to one of its insiders. Hence, for example, the home mortgage assistance programs formerly run by many employers in high-cost locations (like Silicon Valley) are no longer permitted.

Restrictions on Trading by Officers

Federal law prohibits insider trading by employees, officers, and directors, among others, of the corporation that issued the stock being traded. Not all insider transactions are illegal, of course. Instead, insider trading is banned only when the insider trades while in possession, and on the basis, of material nonpublic information. Information is material for this purpose if there is a substantial likelihood that a reasonable investor would consider the information important in deciding how to act. Information remains nonpublic until it is disclosed in a manner that ensures its availability to the investing public. Merely waiting until a press release is read to reporters at a news conference, for example, is not enough. The information must have been widely disseminated and public investors must have an opportunity to act on it.

As a matter of good corporate practice, all publicly held corporations should adopt policies designed to prevent illegal trading by insiders. Such policies protect the insiders by providing guidance as to when trading is least likely to result in liability. Given the severe penalties for inside trading, and the inevitable temptation to profit from access to inside information, such policies are necessary to, in a sense, protect insiders from themselves. Equally important, moreover, such policies also protect the issuer itself from potential liability.

WHEN TO CALL THE LAWYER

If you are a so-called § 16 insider—a person who owns more than 10 percent of the company's stock, a director, or officer (including vice presidents and others with policy-making functions)—you should generally consult company counsel before selling stock to ensure that you comply not only with SOX but also the various other federal restrictions on insider transactions.

An effective blackout policy obviously must preclude insiders from trading stock they hold directly. In order to ensure compliance, however, it should also apply to stock held indirectly, such as stock held in a 401(k) or other employee benefit program.

Abuse of just such a blackout policy was one of the most unsavory features of the Enron scandal. As Enron was going down the tubes, rank-and-file Enron employees were prevented from selling Enron stock held in their 401(k) plans during a lengthy blackout period imposed while the plan changed administrators. At the same time, however, top Enron executives were selling large amounts of stock they owned directly.

SOX § 306 was adopted in direct response to this part of the Enron saga. Under it, directors and executive officers of a corporation are forbidden from trading any of their company's equity securities during any blackout period in which 50 percent or more of the issuer's employees are banned from trading stocks held in pension and benefit accounts. In addition, subject to some minor exceptions, employees must be given thirty days notice before a blackout period commences.

If an executive officer or director violates the trading ban, the company can sue to recover any profit the executive earns from the trade. If the company fails to do so, § 306 expressly authorizes shareholders of the company to sue derivatively on the company's behalf to force the executive to disgorge profits.

Accelerated Reporting of Insider Transactions

Certain high-ranking corporate insiders are subject to a special set of anti-insider trading rules under § 16 of the Securities Exchange Act. Section 16(b) provides that any profits a covered insider earns on purchases and sales that occur within six months of each other must be turned over to the corporation. Section 16(a) requires covered insiders to file with the SEC a Form 4 on which they report their purchases and sales of company stock. The insiders subject to these requirements are shareholders who own more than 10 percent of the company's stock, members of the board of directors, and officers of the company.

WHO IS AN OFFICER?

Securities Exchange Act Rule 16a-1(f) states:

> The term "officer" shall mean an issuer's president, principal financial officer, principal accounting officer (or, if there is no such accounting officer, the controller), any vice-president of the issuer in charge of a principal business unit, division or function (such as sales, administration or finance), any other officer who performs a policy-making function, or any other person who performs similar policy-making functions for the issuer.

Someone who holds one of the listed titles is likely to be deemed an officer, whether or not he or she has access to inside information, subject to a "very limited exception applicable only where the title is essentially honorary or ceremonial." (Conversely, the mere fact that one's position is described in, say, the corporate bylaws as that of an officer does not suffice to make one an officer for this purpose.) An executive with policy-making functions that give the executive access to inside information, however, is an officer even if the executive lacks one of the formal titles usually associated with that position.

Pre-SOX, executives filed a Form 4 within ten days after the end of any month in which the executive purchased or sold some of his company's stock. Under SOX, reporting must take place much more quickly. The executive now must file a Form 4 disclosing his or her trades within two business days following the transaction. The form must be filed electronically and a copy posted to the company's Web site within one day after it is filed with the SEC.

Note that only transactions in stock of the executive's company have to be disclosed. Let's say you're an executive of Acme. You own a bunch of stock in Ajax. You're not an officer, director, or more than 10 percent shareholder of Ajax. You can buy or sell Ajax stock without having to file a Form 4.

WHEN TO SEE A LAWYER

There are complicated rules governing disclosure of stock options and convertible securities. You should check with company counsel or benefits personnel before purchasing, selling, or otherwise receiving or disposing of, options and/or convertible bonds.

Shareholder Vote on Executive Compensation

Shareholders long have been required to vote on some types of executive compensation, especially those involving stock options or other stock grants to executives. In order for a stock option program to qualify as an Incentive Stock Option plan (ISO) and thus receive favorable tax treatment, for example, the shareholders must approve the plan. Likewise, a stock option plan approved by the shareholders gets an exemption from the prohibition on short-swing profits under § 16(b) (see the preceding section).

As part of its post-Enron changes to the Listed Company Manual, the NYSE adopted a new requirement that stockholders "must be given the opportunity to vote on all equity-compensation plans and material revisions thereto." Any arrangement by which equity securities—common stock, preferred stock, or convertible bonds—of the listed company are provided to any employee, director, or other provider of services as compensation is covered. "Even a compensatory grant of options or other equity securities that is not made under a plan is, nonetheless, an 'equity-compensation plan' for these purposes." Plans that are open to other shareholders (such as dividend reinvestment plans) or stock purchase plans under which an employee can buy stock at the fair market value are exempted.

Document Retention and Destruction

In Enron and many of the other corporate governance scandals, there was rampant obstruction of justice. Indeed, in some cases, such as that against Martha Stewart, obstruction charges ended up being the principal grounds on which the defendant was indicted.

SOX added a number of new or modified antiobstruction provisions to the criminal code. First, an existing obstruction of justice provision (§ 1520 of the U.S. Criminal Code) was amended to close a loophole. Pre-SOX, the statute did not apply to an individual who destroys documents while acting alone. SOX changed the statute to prohibit document destruction even by a single individual. The defendant can be held liable for destroying documents even if there has not yet been a grand jury subpoena seeking the documents, but the defendant must have acted with intent to obstruct an investigation in order to be held liable.

Second, there are stiff criminal penalties for anyone who "knowingly alters, destroys, mutilates, conceals, covers up, falsifies, or makes a false entry in any record, document, or tangible object with the intent to impede, obstruct, or influence the investigation or proper administration of any matter within the jurisdiction of any department or agency of the United States or any case filed under [the Bankruptcy Code]." Note that this provision is one of the two sections of SOX directly applicable to nonprofit organizations and closely held corporations. Finally, there are new rules requiring auditors to retain audit-related documents for up to seven years.

WHEN TO CALL IN THE LAWYERS

There is no one-size-fits-all solution to creating document retention policies. Attorney John P. Hutchins correctly explains that "the content and operation of an effective document retention policy will vary from company to company—and even from business unit to business unit within a company—depending on the primary business objectives of the organization, the main goals of the document retention policy and the practices followed by the organization to successfully mesh the business objectives with the implementation of the policy." Consult with competent counsel before finalizing any document retention policy.

A best practice approach to document retention includes:

- Development of written document retention policies. The company must communicate the policies to all employees, not just those whose job description includes responsibility for the company's books or records. After all, in many workplaces, practically every employee has one of the most effective document retention devices ever invented sitting on his or her desk: a computer.
- The company should develop processes for central storage and easy retrieval of those documents and records that make up the company's core institutional memory.

- Processes should be developed to ensure that documents that are no longer needed for either business or legal reasons are routinely destroyed. The procedures need to include such items as removal of e-mail from hard drives and other oft-overlooked locations in which document copies might inadvertently be stored.
- Prohibit destruction or alteration of documents if litigation or a government investigation is brought or even rumored.

When in doubt remember the old line about Watergate: It's not the crime, it's the cover-up. Document destruction or alteration is tempting when one is staring down the barrel of an investigation, as Martha Stewart proved when she started tinkering with her old phone message slips, but it's dumb. With the proliferation of document copies across computer networks and the advanced forensics available to law enforcement, destroying or altering documents is a losing proposition.

4

Whistle Blowers, Lawyers, and the Costs of Misconduct

Part of the Enron mythology is that former Enron VP Sherron Watkins blew the whistle on Ken Lay, Jeff Skilling, and their fellow miscreants. In fact, as *Time* magazine explained:

> In the news media, it is "Enron whistle-blower" Sherron Watkins, even though Watkins never really blew a whistle. A whistle-blower would have written that letter to the *Houston Chronicle*, and long before August; Watkins wrote it to Ken Lay, and warned him of potential whistle-blowers lurking among them. (She quotes one of them as lamenting, "We're such a crooked company.")

Nevertheless, by the time Congress started work on SOX, this myth of the brave employee bringing down an evil corporate empire had taken root. In order to protect those who blew the whistle on firms like Enron and WorldCom, as well as to encourage future whistle blowers, Congress included two sets of protections for whistle blowers in SOX: (1) Criminal penalties for those who retaliate against whistle blowers and (2) civil remedies for whistle blowers who are fired or otherwise suffer some form of retaliation by their employer.

What Is Whistle Blowing?

Lawyers don't use the term *whistle blowing;* instead, they talk about "protected activity." In other words, what actions by an employee may an employer not properly punish?

SOX § 806 identifies a number of actions that employers may not retaliate against or otherwise punish an employee for taking, including:

- Providing information to, or otherwise assisting, an investigation of wire, mail, or bank fraud, or any other federal law on fraud against shareholders, or other securities law violations. Investigations by the SEC, other federal regulatory or law enforcement agencies, and Congress are covered by this provision. It also applies, however, to internal investigations by the employee's supervisors or any company employee having responsibility for investigating misconduct. In particular, the provision thus covers the company's internal audit personnel and members of the audit committee of the board of directors. Note that there need not be a pre-existing investigation for the employee to be engaged in protected activity. An employee who makes an internal or external complaint about alleged fraud violations is protected.
- Filing, testifying, participating in, or otherwise assisting in any legal proceeding involving fraud or other securities violations by the company.

In order to encourage whistle blowing, the Department of Labor has issued an interpretation of § 806 pursuant to which an employee who reports conduct he or she reasonably believes is a violation of one of the covered federal fraud or securities laws is engaged in protected activity even if subsequent investigation proves the employee was wrong. This makes sense, of course. Would employees come forward with charges of serious misconduct if they know they can be fired if they turn out to have made a mistake? On the other hand, however, it means companies likely will face many more whistle-blowing complaints.

The employee need not specify which laws he or she thinks are being broken. Instead, it is enough that the employee generically allege fraud or other securities misconduct. On the other hand, as one court recently explained, there must be "allegations of conduct that would alert" the employer that the employee "believed the company was violating any federal rule or law related to fraud on shareholders." Note that the employee's belief that laws are being violated has both an objective and a subjective component. In other words, the employee must actually believe one or more of the requisite laws is being violated and that belief must be reasonable.

What Is Retaliation?

Lawyers don't talk about retaliation or punishment; instead, they talk about adverse employment action (or adverse action, for short). This is so because the range of prohibited employer conduct taken against those who engage in protected activity is so broad. Adverse actions clearly include threats, reprimands, job transfers, pay cuts, or other actions having a negative effect on employment conditions.

Other types of employer action are subject to more uncertainty. There's disagreement, for example, as to whether negative performance evaluations constitute adverse employment action if the evaluation does not result in a lower salary, directly jeopardize the employee's job security, or otherwise cause any tangible job detriment.

An important emerging issue is whether creating a hostile working environment for SOX whistle blowers constitutes adverse employment action. Most employers are all too well acquainted with court rulings that a hostile working environment for, say, minorities or women can constitute illegal discrimination based on race or gender. Most observers expect a similar development to protect SOX whistle blowers. Hence, an employee subjected to intentional harassment because of protected activity, which is sufficiently severe or pervasive as to create a hostile working environment, and which detrimentally affected the employee and would have detrimentally affected a reasonable person, likely has suffered an adverse action.

Criminal Penalties

SOX § 1107 creates a criminal penalty of up to ten years imprisonment and/or a fine of up to $250,000 on anyone who intentionally retaliates against a whistle blower by taking "any action harmful to any person, including interference with the lawful employment or livelihood of any person." Along with the document destruction prohibition discussed in the preceding section, this is one of the two SOX provisions directly applicable to nonprofit organizations and closely held corporations.

Civil Penalties

SOX § 806 authorizes whistle blowers who suffer retaliation to seek back pay, reinstatement, and compensatory damages from the company. Unlike the criminal sanctions, the civil remedies under § 806 are limited mainly to employees of reporting companies. In addition, however, privately held companies providing services to a reporting company as a contractor, subcontractor, or agent are subject to § 806.

WHAT ABOUT SUBSIDIARIES?

Many corporations are part of a larger corporate group. Obviously, employees who work directly for a publicly traded parent corporation are protected by § 806. Likewise, employees are also covered by § 806 if they work for a subsidiary that is a reporting company either because it has some public shareholders or publicly traded debt as to which it must file annual and quarterly reports. Courts are divided, however, as to whether employees who work for nonpublicly traded subsidiaries of a reporting company are covered. Finally, at least one court has held that a foreign employee of a subsidiary incorporated in a foreign country is not protected by § 806 even if the parent corporation is a U.S. reporting company.

SOX assigned responsibility for dealing with complaints of adverse action against whistle blowers to the Department of Labor (DOL), which in turn has assigned the job to the Occupational Safety and Health Administration (OSHA). Under § 806 and the rules adopted by OSHA, an employee who wants to complain of adverse action must do so within ninety days of the action about which he or she wants to complain. OSHA then has sixty days to conduct an investigation. While OSHA is conducting its investigation, the employer has twenty days from the time it becomes aware of the complaint to file written submissions with OSHA and/or request a meeting with the OSHA investigator. In addition, if OSHA is preparing to issue a finding adverse to the employer, it will give the employer another chance to present its case before closing the investigation.

If OSHA concludes that there is reasonable cause to believe the employee suffered prohibited adverse action, it will authorize the employee to bring a case against the employer before a DOL administrative law judge (ALJ). Whichever side loses before the ALJ can appeal to the DOL's Administrative Review Board. Whichever side loses before the board may take an appeal to federal court.

In practice, the OSHA procedure rarely reaches a conclusion. Section 806 provides that if the DOL does not issue a final decision within 180 days after the employee files the complaint, the employee may bring suit against the employer in federal district court. As labor law attorney Eugene Scalia (son of U.S. Supreme Court Justice Antonin Scalia) observes in an article on Sarbanes-Oxley and whistle-blower protection:

> One hundred and eighty days is not nearly enough time for an OSHA investigation and decision letter; discovery; trial before an administrative law judge; post-trial briefing; issuance of the ALJ decision; and, possibly, briefing and review before the ARB. As a practical matter, then, complainants will usually have the opportunity to go to federal court, although for a variety of reasons they may choose to remain before the Labor Department.

Whether the suit goes forward before a DOL ALJ or a federal trial judge, the initial burden is on the employee to show by a preponderance of the evidence that the employee's protected activity was a "contributing factor" in the employer's decision to take adverse action against the employee. If the employee does so, the burden shifts to the defendant employer to show by clear and convincing evidence that the employer would have taken the adverse employment action without regard to the employee's protected activity. In other words, the employer must show that the disciplinary action was taken for reasons other than the employee having blown the whistle.

PARDON MY LEGALISMS

In litigation, the burden of proof—that is, the duty to persuade the judge or jury that he or she should win—normally is on the plaintiff. In some legal contexts, however, if the plaintiff can make out a preliminary showing that the defendant did something wrong, the burden of proof shifts to the defendant.

Not only does the burden of proof sometimes shift from one side of the case to the other, the amount of evidence the side with the burden of proof has to provide can also vary.

Sometimes the side with the burden of proof has to have the "preponderance of the evidence," which means its evidence must be more credible and convincing than the other side's, such that it is more probable than not that the side with the burden of proof has the better case. In some cases, however, such as SOX § 806, the side with the burden of proof has a more exacting task of showing "clear and convincing evidence." Under this standard, it must be substantially more likely than not that the side with the burden of proof has the better case.

A Best Practice Approach to Whistle Blowing

According to the IT Compliance Institute, an industry trade association, "of the 223 cases filed under the whistle-blower provisions of Sarbanes-Oxley through August 2004, all but eight (97 percent) were dropped or otherwise not acted on, including one that involved severe data security violations." Although it thus may seem like companies face little risk, most lawyers and corporate governance consultants advise that companies nevertheless take a best practice approach to dealing with actual or potential whistle blowers. While few complaints may have succeeded, the number of retaliation complaints filed by purported whistle blowers has steadily increased in the last five years. The liability exposure for improperly handling whistle blower complaints thus is significant.

The critical first step in setting up a process for handling whistle blower complaints is complying with Sarbanes-Oxley § 301's requirement that the audit committee of every reporting company must establish a system for receiving, documenting, and processing complaints about the company's accounting, internal controls, or auditing. The system must provide for confidential and anonymous submission of employee complaints about questionable accounting or auditing matters.

In setting up such a system, employers can take advantage of the fact that SOX built on existing protections for whistle blowers in many other employment areas. The retaliation provisions of Title VII, the ADEA, the ADA, and the Equal Pay Act, for example, long have prohibited retaliation against an employee or applicant who opposed an unlawful employment practice, made a complaint, or testified, assisted, or otherwise participated in an investigation or legal proceeding. Employer policies designed to prevent retaliation in these areas thus can be adapted to add SOX protections.

A best practice policy will include:

- A written policy statement banning retaliation in any way against whistle blowers. In particular, the policy statement should state that employees reporting violations will be protected from retaliation.

- The policy statement should clearly articulate the company's complaint mechanism, including procedures for submitting anonymous complaints. The policy should identify those managers to whom complaints can be reported and discussed. (It may be appropriate to establish a corporate compliance officer to oversee all of the company's whistle-blowing policies and complaint procedures, as well as to take responsibility for ensuring that the firm complies with all relevant laws and regulations.)
- In developing both the complaint mechanism and the policy statement, the company should use a multidisciplinary team, in which corporate counsel has primary responsibility, but input is received from all key business unit heads, as well as top management of the finance, accounting, human resources, and internal audit departments. Adopting such a team approach will help ensure that the policy reflects the needs and advice of the units in which complaints are most likely to arise.
- The policy should be distributed to all employees, probably as part of an employment manual.
- The firm should provide training for managers and supervisors on avoiding actions that might be deemed retaliatory.
- Careful supervision by human resources and/or legal counsel of any job-related actions taken with respect to the whistle blower until the matter is fully resolved.

Any complaint received should be fully documented, even if it is immediately apparent to the investigator that no violation occurred. The documentation should memorialize the actions the employer took to investigate and resolve the complaint. Any actions taken that affect the complaining employee must be particularly well documented.

A particularly serious problem arises when poor job performance coincides with an employee whistle-blowing complaint. In some cases, a poorly performing employee might file a SOX § 806 complaint as a strategic maneuver to prevent the employer from taking disciplinary action. In others, an employee's supervisors might cobble together charges of poor performance in order to discredit a whistle blower. Finally, a lousy employee might have legitimate charges to bring.

Because SOX exposes employers and managers to the risk of criminal sanctions and/or having to pay large monetary damages, attorney fees, as well as the need to reinstate terminated employees, the safest approach is to treat all complaints as legitimate even if the employee in question has a known pattern of poor performance. In order to ensure that disciplinary action may be taken against a poorly performing employee who has also engaged in protected activity, the employer must be able to clearly document that the complaint was not a contributing factor in the decision to take disciplinary action. Providing employees with regular, written performance evaluations will help establish the necessary paper record. (Managers and supervisors should be trained to avoid criticism of an employee's protected activity in performance evaluations.) Advice from legal counsel and/or human resources personnel should be sought before taking any disciplinary action.

Managing the Lawyer-Client Relationship Post-SOX

While Sarbanes-Oxley provides significant protections for whistle blowers, it leaves the decision to blow the whistle up to the employee in most cases. One category of employees and agents, however, is now obligated to blow the whistle on securities violations. The company's lawyers, whether inside counsel or an outside law firm service provider, are obliged by SOX and SEC rules to report securities violations up the corporate ladder to top management and, in some cases, the board of directors.

Where Were the Lawyers?

In rendering a legal opinion arising out of the 1980s Lincoln Savings & Loan scandal, Judge (and former SEC Director of Enforcement) Stanley Sporkin famously observed:

> Where were these professionals, a number of whom are now asserting their rights under the Fifth Amendment, when these clearly improper transactions were being consummated? Why didn't any of them speak up or disassociate themselves from the transactions? Where also were the outside accountants and attorneys when these transactions were effectuated? What is difficult to understand is that with all the professional talent involved (both accounting and legal), why at least one professional would not have blown the whistle to stop the overreaching that took place in this case. *Lincoln Sav. & Loan Ass'n v. Wall,* 743 F. Supp. 901, 920 (D.D.C. 1990).

A decade or so later, the same questions were asked of lawyers who worked for firms like Enron.

There is little doubt that lawyers played an important role in the scandals. Sometimes their negligence allowed management misconduct to go undetected. Sometimes lawyers even acted as facilitators and enablers of management impropriety. According to Enron's internal investigation, for example, there "was an absence of forceful and effective oversight [of the company's disclosures] by . . . in-house counsel, and objective and critical professional advice by outside counsel at Vinson & Elkins," along with senior management and the auditors. The report expressly criticized Vinson & Elkins, which the investigators argued "should have brought a stronger, more objective and more critical voice to the disclosure process."

In the floor debate over Sarbanes-Oxley, Senator John Edwards (D-NC) summed up the problem by concluding that when "executives and/or accountants are breaking the law, you can be sure that part of the problem is that the lawyers who are there and involved are not doing their jobs." Edwards further argued that after "all the . . . corporate misconduct we have seen, it is . . . clear that corporate lawyers should not be left to regulate themselves no more than accountants should be left to regulate themselves." Accordingly, he proposed an amendment, subsequently enacted as § 307 of the act, requiring the SEC to:

> [I]issue rules . . . setting forth minimum standards of professional conduct for attorneys appearing and practicing before the Commission in any way in the representation of issuers, including a rule—(1) requiring an attorney to report evidence of a material violation of securities law or breach of fiduciary duty or similar violation by the company or any agent thereof, to the chief legal counsel or the chief executive officer of the company (or the equivalent thereof); and (2) if the counsel or officer does not appropriately respond to the evidence . . . requiring the attorney to report the evidence to the audit committee of the board of directors of the issuer or to another committee of the board of directors comprised solely of directors not employed . . . by the issuer, or to the board of directors.

Up-the-Ladder Reporting

Edwards explained that § 307 was intended to give lawyers a very "simple" obligation: "You report the violation. If the violation isn't addressed properly, then you go to the board." Note the emphasis on reporting to the board. Like so many of Sarbanes-Oxley's provisions, § 307 clearly is directed at enhancing the role of the board vis-à-vis that of management.

In response to § 307, the SEC in January 2003 promulgated attorney conduct regulations. At the heart of these so-called "Part 205" regulations is a version of the up-the-ladder reporting requirement envisioned by Senator Edwards.

The rules apply only to a lawyer who is "appearing and practicing before the Commission in the representation of an issuer." Unfortunately, the definition of "appearing and practicing" is both sweeping and quite vague, which is an ugly combination. As a result, many nonsecurities lawyers are surprised to find that they must comply with the Part 205 regulations.

In particular, the applicable rule provides, in pertinent part, that:

> Appearing and practicing before the Commission: (1) Means: . . . Providing advice in respect of the United States securities laws or the Commission's rules or regulations thereunder regarding any document that the attorney has notice will be filed with or submitted to, or incorporated into any document that will be filed with or submitted to, the Commission, including the provision of such advice in the context of preparing, or participating in the preparation of, any such document.

To be sure, the SEC has advised that "an attorney's preparation of a document (such as a contract) which he or she never intended or had notice would be submitted to the Commission, or incorporated into a document submitted to the Commission, but which subsequently is submitted to the Commission as an exhibit to or in connection with a filing, does not constitute 'appearing and practicing' before the Commission." Yet, many nonsecurities lawyers may know that their documents are filed and thus will find themselves "appearing and practicing" before the Commission.

Once it is determined that a given attorney is "appearing and practicing" before the SEC, that attorney "owes his or her professional and ethical duties to the issuer as an organization." The Part 205 regulations further emphasize that the attorney "represents the issuer as an entity rather than the officers." The idea here is to ensure that the lawyer takes actions that are in the best interests of the organization rather than looking out for the interests of top management.

Frankly, it may be doubted just how effective this admonition will prove in practice. Young lawyers quickly learn that to advance they must develop a set of skills and attitudes aimed squarely at keeping clients happy. Survey data confirms that the ability to develop "good working relationships with clients and peers" is a highly ranked consideration in the decision by a law firm to promote a young lawyer to partnership. Another highly ranked consideration is "a willingness to pursue the interests of clients aggressively."

While in theory the client is the organization, lawyers know that the corporation is just a legal fiction. The real client is the person or persons with the power to hire or fire the lawyer. Because it is top management—not the board of directors—that hires both the internal general counsel and outside lawyers, it is management whom attorneys must please in order to retain or attract business. This pressure is especially true given the large number of capable firms and attorneys available for hire; law firms are something akin to a fungible good. In addition, legal counsel normally works far more closely with senior management than with the board of directors. Senator Edwards aptly explained the net effect of these factors during the floor debate over Sarbanes-Oxley:

We have seen corporate lawyers sometimes forget who their client is. What happens is their day-to-day conduct is with the CEO or the chief financial officer because those are the individuals responsible for hiring them. So as a result, that is with whom they have a relationship. When they go to lunch with their client, the corporation, they are usually going to lunch with the CEO or the chief financial officer. When they get phone calls, they are usually returning calls to the CEO or the chief financial officer.

The bare reality is that SOX has not changed that dynamic.

In any case, the initial obligation of a lawyer who "becomes aware of evidence of a material violation by the issuer or by any officer, director, employee, or agent of the issuer" is to report such evidence to the issuer's chief legal or executive officer. The lawyer need not cry wolf every time there is the slightest hint of a possible problem, however. Instead, the lawyer's reporting obligation is triggered only by "credible evidence" that would lead a prudent and competent attorney to believe it is "reasonably likely" that a material violation has taken place, is taking place at present, or will occur in the near future. (Actually, the precise standard set out in the rules is a mess of legal gobbledygook with lots of double negatives, but the foregoing is close enough for our purposes.)

Subject to a slew of exceptions and alternatives, unless the lawyer "reasonably believes that [that officer] has provided an appropriate response within a reasonable time, the attorney shall report the evidence of a material violation to" the audit committee of the board of directors. The lawyer must report both violations of federal securities law and state fiduciary duties.

An "appropriate response" is defined by Part 205 as a response that leads the attorney to reasonably believe that: (1) There is no material violation; (2) there was a material violation, but the company has taken appropriate remedial measures; or (3) that the company has retained or directed an attorney to investigate the report and has been advised by such attorney that there is a colorable defense to the alleged violation. The SEC has emphasized that attorneys are free to exercise their own judgment as to whether a response is an appropriate one, so long as their judgment is a reasonable one.

The Part 205 regulations permit a company to establish a so-called "qualified legal compliance committee" (QLCC) composed of at least two or more independent directors, at least one of whom must be a member of the audit committee of the board of directors. The QLCC is tasked with receiving and investigating complaints by in-house or outside counsel of possible material violations. Many companies are using their audit committee as the QLCC, although this has the disadvantage of piling yet another task on the increasingly overworked shoulders of the audit committee.

The advantage of using the QLCC process is that an attorney who makes a report to the QLCC has satisfied his or her reporting obligation and, most importantly, is not required to assess the QLCC's response. In addition, a general counsel who receives a report of a material violation can buck the report to the QLCC instead of conducting an individual investigation.

There are a couple of important restrictions on the use of a QLCC. First, the QLCC may only deal with reports that are received after it has been established. In other words, if a report is already working its way up the ladder, it's too late to set up a QLCC to deal with that report. Second, the QLCC can't just brush the report under the rug. The QLCC must adopt a written policy for how it will handle any report of a possible material violation. The QLCC must be empowered to conduct an investigation, to recommend that the board of directors and/or management take remedial measures, and be authorized to notify the SEC if the board of directors and top management fail to implement appropriate remedial measures. Lastly, the QLCC is required to notify the board, CEO, and the general counsel of the results of any investigation and any remedial measures imposed or proposed.

Blowing the Whistle Externally

In promulgating the Part 205 regulations, the SEC considered imposing an obligation for counsel to blow the whistle by reporting securities violations to the SEC and/or law enforcement. Under the proposed rule, an attorney whose internal complaints were not met with an adequate mitigating response by the issuer would be obliged to resign from the corporation and to file a notification with the SEC explaining the basis for such resignation. The proposal met with savage criticism from both the legal profession and the business community. The principal objection was that such a requirement would force lawyers to disclose client confidences.

Unlike the much-debated noisy withdrawal issue, an up-the-ladder reporting requirement does not require the lawyer to violate client confidences. Because an attorney's client is the corporate entity, rather than an individual employee or group of employees, discussing client information with anyone authorized to make decisions within the organization is not a breach of confidence. Indeed, the Part 205 regulations make this point explicit: "By communicating such information [i.e., about securities violations] to the issuer's officers or directors, an attorney does not reveal client confidences or secrets."

Although noisy withdrawal is not required, it is permitted under certain circumstances. A lawyer may disclose client confidences to the SEC or law enforcement where such disclosure is necessary:

- To help the lawyer defend him- or herself in an investigation or proceeding in which the attorney's compliance with SEC rules and the up-the-ladder reporting requirement is at issue
- To prevent the company from committing a material violation of the securities laws that is likely to cause substantial injury to the financial interests or assets of the company or shareholders
- To rectify a material violation by the company that caused substantial injury to the company's financial interests or assets or those of its shareholders if the attorney's services were used in furtherance of the violation
- To prevent the company from committing perjury or otherwise working a fraud on the SEC

Best Practices for Dealing with Lawyers Post-SOX

There's a very real risk that the new post-SOX legal ethics rules will make the lawyer-client relationship more adversarial and less productive. The keep-the-client-happy mentality discussed above long inclined counsel to overlook—whether intentionally or subconsciously—evidence of management misconduct. Sarbanes-Oxley did not address those incentives. Indeed, while it is intended to create counterincentives in the form of potential disciplinary proceedings, § 307 may have the unintended consequence of actually encouraging lawyers to turn a blind eye to corporate problems. Under the Part 205 regulations, an attorney is only responsible for material violations of which he or she "becomes aware." As such, the rational lawyer has yet another rationale for closing his or her eyes to potential misconduct. Avoiding detailed information about clients' conduct is one way of avoiding even the risk of incurring a duty to report or any subsequent liability exposure. As corporate law expert Larry Ribstein therefore explained: "The new rules may inhibit even innocuous conversations that might have helped indirectly in uncovering frauds by making them fodder for federal litigation and investigations."

On the other side of the equation, corporate managers will not welcome the kind of investigation that an attorney's "reporting up" would engender. Even a mistaken accusation of wrongdoing by an attorney could have adverse consequences for the implicated managers. As a result, managers may be tempted to minimize the overall amount of information to which an attorney has access ("just to be on the safe side"). Indeed, managers will be tempted to shield their lawyers from information not only about potential wrongdoing but also about legal but aggressive—envelope-pushing—accounting and disclosure practices.

Such a deterioration in the lawyer-client relationship would be most unfortunate. Corporate lawyers are one of the basic categories of advisors who play a critical role in virtually all corporate transactions. But why?

The reason people hire litigators is obvious—either they are being sued or they want to sue somebody else. Unauthorized practice of law statutes and bar admission rules give lawyers a near-total monopoly on litigation.

The rationale for hiring transactional lawyers, by contrast, is less obvious. Much of the work of transactional lawyers entails giving advice that could be given by other professionals. Accordingly, it seems fair to ask: Why does anybody hire transactional lawyers?

Two competing hypotheses suggest themselves. The first might be termed the "Pie-Division Role." In this version of the transactional lawyer story, lawyers strive to capture value—maximizing their client's gains from the deal. Although there are doubtless pie-division situations in transactional practice, this explanation of the lawyer's role is flawed. Pie division assumes a zero-sum game in which any gains for one side come from the other side's share. Assume two sophisticated clients with multiple advisors, including competent counsel. Is there any reason to think that one side's lawyer will be able to extract significant gains from the other? No. A homely example may be helpful: You and a friend go out to eat. You decide to share a pizza, so you need to agree on its division. Would you hire somebody to negotiate a division of the pizza? Especially if they were going to take one of your slices as their fee?

The second hypothesis might be termed the "Pie-Expansion Role." In this version of the story, people hire transactional lawyers because they add value to the deal. This conception of the lawyer's role rejects the zero-sum game mentality. Instead, it claims that the lawyer makes everybody better off by increasing the size of the pie.

For the most part, lawyers increase the size of the pie by reducing transaction costs. One way of lowering transaction cost is through regulatory arbitrage. The law frequently provides multiple ways of effecting a given transaction, all of which will have various advantages and disadvantages. By selecting the most advantageous structure for a given transaction, and ensuring that courts and regulators will respect that choice, the transactional lawyer reduces the cost of complying with the law and allows the parties to keep more of their gains.

An example may be helpful. Acme Corporation wants to acquire Ajax, Inc., using stock as the form of consideration to be paid Ajax shareholders. Acme is concerned about the availability of appraisal rights to shareholders of the two corporations. Presumably Acme doesn't care about the legal niceties of doing the deal—Acme just wants to buy Ajax at the lowest possible cost and, by hypothesis, with the minimal possible cash flow. In other words, the client cares about the economic substance of the deal, not the legal form it takes. As Acme's transactional lawyer, you know that corporate law often elevates form over substance—and that the law provides multiple ways of acquiring another company. A solution thus suggests itself: Delaware law only permits shareholders to exercise appraisal rights in connection with mergers. Appraisal rights are not allowed in connection with an acquisition structured as a sale of assets. Hence, while there is no substantive economic difference between an asset sale and a merger, there is a significant legal difference. By selecting one form over another, the transactional lawyer ensures that the deal is done at the lowest possible cost.

Parties would experience some transaction costs even in the absence of regulation, however. Reducing those nonregulatory costs is another function of the transactional lawyer. Information asymmetries are a good example. A corporation selling securities to an investor has considerably greater information about the firm than does the prospective buyer. The wise potential investor knows about this information asymmetry and, as a result, takes precautions. Worse yet, what if the seller lies? Or shades the truth? Or is itself uninformed? The wise investor also knows there is a risk of opportunistic withholding or manipulation of asymmetrically held information. One response is investigation—due diligence—by the buyer. Another response is for the seller to provide disclosures including representations and warranties. In either case, by finding ways for the seller to convey credibly information to the investor, the transactional lawyer helps eliminate the information asymmetry between them. In turn, a variety of other transaction costs will fall. There is less uncertainty, less opportunity for strategic behavior, and less need to take costly precautions.

To ensure that the client gets the full benefit of these transactional lawyering services, the firm and counsel need to develop jointly a best practice approach to dealing with possible material violations. In consultation with the audit committee or QLCC, the general counsel and principal outside counsel should develop a written policy for identifying and reporting violations. The board members, CEO, and CFO should be briefed on their legal obligations with respect to reports, but also encouraged to view a report as a potential win-win situation rather than a zero-sum or adversarial game. Up-the-ladder reporting can give the firm an opportunity to cut off potential violations before they mature into a legal or public relations nightmare, but only if counsel and managers are willing to trust one another.

Expanded Liabilities

SOX significantly ramped up the cost of corporate misconduct. Many existing penalties were toughened. A number of new civil liabilities and criminal penalties for both individuals and corporate entities were created. We just saw two important sets: those relating to document destruction and whistle blowing. In this section, we examine the other principal new liabilities created by SOX.

False Certifications

As we've seen, SOX § 906 mandates that the CEO and CFO certify that the information contained in the company's periodic reports fairly and accurately presents the company's financial condition and results of operations. Anyone who files such a certification knowing that the statement does not comply with those requirements can be fined up to $1 million and/or imprisoned for up to ten years. Anyone who *willfully* files such a certification knowing that the statement does not comply with those requirements can be fined up to $5 million and/or imprisoned for up to twenty years.

Attorney Gerald Walpin, in a memorandum on criminal penalties and SOX § 906, explains:

> It is apparent that the authors of this legislation were relying on Supreme Court definitions, in other contexts, of the elements of "knowingly" and "willfully." Thus, the Supreme Court explained that "the term 'knowingly' does not necessarily have any reference to a culpable state of mind or to knowledge of the law"; rather "'the knowledge requisite to knowing violation of a statute is factual knowledge as distinguished from knowledge of the law.'" . . . In contrast, "willfully" requires proof "that the defendant acted with an evil-meaning mind, that is to say, that he acted with knowledge that his conduct was unlawful."

In other words, knowing that the certification doesn't fairly present the company's financial conditions and results of operations gets you ten years, while knowing that certification violates the law gets you twenty. In short, don't file a 906 certification unless, to the best of your knowledge, it fairly and accurately presents the company's financial condition and results of operations.

Bars on Service as a Director or Officer

The SEC long has had authority to seek court orders barring persons who violate the securities laws from serving as officers or directors of public corporations. In order to obtain such an order, the SEC had to persuade the court that the individual's conduct demonstrated "substantial unfitness" to serve in one of those capacities.

SOX expanded the SEC's powers here in two significant ways. First, the SEC now may impose such a bar without going to court by bringing an administrative cease and desist proceeding against an individual who committed securities fraud. Second, the standard for imposing such a ban has been reduced to mere "unfitness."

Forfeiture of Bonuses and Profits

As we saw in Chapter 1, one of the principal political factors driving the passage of Sarbanes-Oxley was the massive wave of corporate earnings restatements in 2000 and 2001. Five years later, we're seeing another massive wave of restatements, this time arising out of SEC investigations into so-called backdated options.

Executive stock options normally carry a strike price equal to the company's stock market price on the date the options were issued. When a corporation backdates an option, it issues the options with a strike price that prevailed on an earlier date. Because the strike price will always be set as of a date on which the company's stock price was lower than the current market price, the option is in the money immediately upon issuance.

Here's an example:

On June 1, 2006, Acme Corporation issued me options on 1,000 shares. The option, however, was dated May 1, 2006, and carried a strike price equal to the May 1 market price of $10 per share. On June 1, the stock price had risen to $15 per share. I exercise the option immediately, paying Acme $10,000 (the $10 strike price times the 1,000 shares I'm buying). I then sell the shares at the market price of $15 per share, for a total of $15,000, realizing a profit of $5,000. (Note that I'm ignoring the complications resulting from the vesting period typically required for compensatory stock options.)

The legal consequences for both corporations and executives of backdating options are severe. Both the company and the executive likely will have to amend their tax returns for relevant years, paying more taxes and penalties. Executives will face criminal and civil fraud charges. Shareholders will sue for securities fraud.

Most important for present purposes, companies often have to restate earnings for the affected years. When option grants are backdated to earlier days when the share price is lower, they effectively become "discount options" that require an expense under accounting rules. For smaller companies that use a lot of options in compensating executives, the restatements often prove to be material.

It's at this point that Sarbanes-Oxley § 304 comes into play. Under § 304, in the event a corporation is obliged to restate its financial statements due to "misconduct," the CEO and CFO must return to the corporation any bonus, incentive, or equity-based compensation they received during the twelve months following the original issuance of the restated financials, along with any profits they realized from the sale of corporate stock during that period.

A wag might call this the "Baldwin Brothers" provision—cute but dumb. Here are just some objections: It pre-empts the board's power over executive compensation. It fails to define the kinds of misconduct that trigger the reimbursement obligation. It requires reimbursement even if others committed the misconduct, with no good faith defense. All of which will tend to encourage CEOs and CFOs to resist restating flawed financial statements and/or to game the timing of their compensation and stock transactions relative to any such restatements.

As of this writing, there have been no attempts to use the § 304 clawback to recapture CEO and CFO compensation.

All the federal cases that have considered the question to date have concluded that there is no private right of action under § 304. In other words, neither the company nor its shareholders can sue under § 304 to force an executive to forfeit performance pay. Instead, it will be up to the SEC to use this tool in enforcement proceedings.

SOX § 1103 provides the SEC with a related tool by allowing the SEC to ask courts to freeze the pay of corporate officers and directors for up to forty-five days during an SEC investigation. If the SEC subsequently sues the target, the pay continues to be held in escrow until the conclusion of the suit. Obviously, the idea here is to prevent the executive from spending or disposing of funds that could be used to reimburse the company or its investors.

5

Reforming the Board of Directors

The corporation's board of directors has many functions. The American Bar Association's authoritative Corporate Director's Guidebook lists nine basic ones:

- Reviewing and monitoring performance of the corporation's business and its operating, financial, and other corporate plans, strategies and objectives, and changing plans and strategies as appropriate;
- Adopting policies of ethical conduct and monitoring compliance with those policies and with applicable laws and regulations;
- Understanding the risk profile of the corporation and reviewing and overseeing risk management programs;
- Understanding the corporation's financial statements and monitoring the adequacy of its financial and other internal controls as well as its disclosure controls and procedures;
- Choosing, setting goals for, regularly evaluating, and establishing the compensation of the chief executive officer and the most senior executives, and making changes in senior management when appropriate;
- Developing, approving, and implementing succession plans for the chief executive officer and the most senior executives;

- Reviewing the process for providing adequate and timely financial and operational information to the corporation's decision makers (including directors) and shareholders;
- Evaluating the procedures, operation, and overall effectiveness of the board and its committees; and
- Establishing the composition of the board and its committees, including choosing director nominees who will bring appropriate expertise and perspectives to the board, recognizing the important role of independent directors.

In practice, we can boil that list down into three core functions: (1) Under all corporation statutes, the board of directors is the key player in the formal decision-making structure. As the Delaware code puts it, for example, the corporation's business and affairs "shall be managed by or under the direction of a board of directors." To be sure, while boards rarely are involved in day-to-day operational decision making, which typically is delegated by the board to managers and other subordinate employees, most boards retain at least some managerial functions. General policy making is commonly a board prerogative, for example. Plus, of course, the board retains the power to hire and fire firm employees—including the CEO—and to define the limits of their authority. (2) The board provides access to a network of contacts that may be useful in gathering resources and/or obtaining business. (3) The board monitors and disciplines top management.

The board's monitoring and oversight function long has been its chief role. SOX and the accompanying changes to the stock exchange listing requirements, however, so emphasized the board's monitoring role as to make it virtually the board's full-time job. Indeed, as the *Wall Street Journal* put it, they "anointed boards of directors, especially 'independent directors' as the capitalist cavalry" to ride to the rescue after Enron.

Board Reform in SOX and the Stock Exchanges

SOX did relatively little to reform boards of directors. Besides some minor tweaking of rules like those governing disclosure of stock transactions by directors and so on, the only substantive changes worked by SOX dealt with the audit committee of the board of directors.

Instead, Congress and the SEC left the heavy lifting on board reform to the stock exchanges. All three major exchanges—the NYSE, NASDAQ, and the American Stock Exchange (AMEX)—amended their corporate governance listing requirements to:

- Require that a majority of the members of the board of directors of most listed companies must be independent of management
- Define independence using very strict bright-line rules
- Expand the duties and powers of the independent directors
- Expand the duties and powers of the audit committee of the board of directors

Although these changes apply only to publicly traded companies having stock listed on one of the three major exchanges, this is one of the areas in which large, privately held corporations and nonprofits have been under particular pressure to become SOX-compliant. Auditors, creditors, and other key stakeholders expect larger firms to, at the very least, create an audit committee composed of outside directors and ensure that at least one member of the audit committee is a financial expert. According to the AICPA, most larger private companies have done so in the last few years.

Director Independence

The close relationship between boards of directors and top management long has aggravated corporate reformers. In his 1976 book, *Taming the Giant Corporation,* for example, Ralph Nader claimed that pollution, workplace hazards, discrimination, unsafe products, corporate crime, and a host of other antisocial corporate behaviors all were attributable to lack of management accountability. In turn, Nader compared directors to "cuckolds," who are "often the last to know when [their] dominant partner—management—has done something illicit."

To redress this situation, Nader called for the institution of full-time professional directors. Incumbent managers could neither sit on the board nor nominate candidates for the board. Once elected, by way of cumulative voting, the board members would serve on a full-time basis, with no outside employment and for no more than four two-year terms. Board members would be provided with staffs and full access to corporate information. Each board member would be responsible for some specified aspect of the business, such as employee welfare or law compliance.

No state corporation code, SEC rule, or stock exchange listing requirement has ever gone as far as Nader wanted. Over the last three decades, however, there has been a growing emphasis on director independence. In other words, there has been growing acceptance of the idea that a substantial number of a corporation's directors should be outsiders who are not beholden to the corporation's CEO or other top managers.

The Majority Independent Board

The NYSE has mandated that all listed companies "must have a majority of independent directors" (NYSE Listed Company Manual § 303A.01). In addition, as we'll see below, the NYSE has mandated the use of several board committees consisting of outsiders. Finally, the NYSE's Listed Company Manual (§ 303A.03) provides that: "To empower non-management directors to serve as a more effective check on management, the non-management directors of each listed company must meet at regularly scheduled executive sessions without management." Although the rule does not indicate how many times per year the outside directors must meet to satisfy this requirement, emerging best practice suggests that there should be such a meeting held in conjunction with every regularly scheduled meeting of the entire board of directors.

REQUIRED DISCLOSURES

The NYSE requires that the identity of the outside directors who chair the mandatory executive sessions must be disclosed in the listed company's Form 10-K. In addition, the Form 10-K or the company's annual proxy statement must include a statement of how interested parties can make concerns known to the outside directors. As a matter of best practice, this requirement should be incorporated into the company's whistle-blower policy.

In July 2006, the SEC amended its disclosure rules to require disclosure of: (1) whether each director and each person nominated to be a director is independent of management; (2) any transactions, arrangements, or other relationships considered by the board of directors in determining if an individual satisfied the applicable independence standards; and (3) identification of any members of the audit, nominating, or compensation committees who are not independent.

The NASDAQ and AMEX standards are substantially similar. One wrinkle is that NASDAQ expressly states an expectation that executive sessions of the outside directors will be held at least twice a year.

Note that both the NYSE and NASDAQ exempt controlled companies—those in which a shareholder or group of shareholders acting together control 50 percent or more of the voting power of the company's stock—from the obligation to have a majority independent board.

Studies of post-SOX boards of directors find that average board size has increased, presumably because companies are adding more independent directors rather than replacing incumbent insiders. Conversely, the average number of companies on whose board a director sits has gone down, presumably because boards and committees meet more often and have to process more information. The amount of time required for board service has especially gone up for members of audit committees, who have a host of new duties.

The cost to the company of all these changes is significant. Director and officer liability insurance policy premiums jumped substantially; according to one study of New York companies, those premiums increased by more than 150 percent from 2001 to 2004. Director compensation keeps going up as well, especially for outside directors on time-consuming committees like the audit committee. The median increase is 56 percent and, according to one study, has been higher for smaller firms: "small firms paid $3.19 in director fees per $1,000 of net sales in 2004, which is $0.84 more than they paid in 2001 and $1.21 more than in 1998."

Who Is Independent?

State corporation law traditionally used a rather vague standard to decide whether a given director was independent of management. As one Delaware judicial opinion put it, the question is whether "through personal or other relationships the directors are beholden to" management. In contrast, the new NYSE and NASDAQ listing requirements adopt strict bright-line rules for deciding whether a director is adequately independent to count toward the requisite majority.

The NYSE Listed Company Manual § 303A.02 sets out a number of tests for determining whether a director is independent. Basically, the rules require that the board of directors determine that a nominee has no material direct or indirect relationship with the listed company. The NYSE cautions that "it is best that boards making 'independence' determinations broadly consider all relevant facts and circumstances. In particular, when assessing the materiality of a director's relationship with the listed company, the board should consider the issue not merely from the standpoint of the director, but also from that of persons or organizations with which the director has an affiliation."

An example might be helpful. Suppose you're the CEO of Acme. Ajax invites you to serve on its board of directors. The Ajax board now must determine whether you'll qualify as independent. In addition to considering your personal relations with Ajax, the Ajax board should also consider the relationship between the two companies. If a large chunk of Acme's business involves working with Ajax, that relationship might affect your judgment, and the Ajax board arguably shouldn't consider you to be independent. In assessing these sorts of relationships, the NYSE advises that: "Material relationships can include commercial, industrial, banking, consulting, legal, accounting, charitable and familial relationships, among others. However, as the concern is independence from management, the Exchange does not view ownership of even a significant amount of stock, by itself, as a bar to an independence finding."

INDEPENDENT VERSUS DISINTERESTED

Just because someone qualifies as independent under the stock exchange definitions doesn't mean that he or she necessarily is disinterested. For example, suppose a member of the board enters into a related-party transaction with the corporation. Even though some such transactions may not disqualify the director from being independent, they still involve a conflict of interest. Thus, our hypothetical director is independent but not disinterested. Only the independent and disinterested directors should act on such transactions. Accordingly, when the board acts on the transaction, the conflicted director should be recused.

The rule further specifies that certain individuals cannot be deemed independent. An employee of the listed company cannot be deemed independent until at least five years after the employment ended. A former affiliate or employee of the listed company's present or former auditor likewise cannot be deemed independent until at least five years after the affiliation or auditing relationship terminated. A director may not be deemed independent if he is employed (or has been employed in the last five years) by a company in which an executive officer of the listed company serves as a member of the board of directors' compensation committee. Directors with immediate family members in any of the foregoing categories are likewise subject to a five-year "cooling-off period."

The director independence rules are a particular area of concern for nonprofits. Suppose you're the CEO of Acme

Corporation. Over the years, Acme has frequently donated money to your alma mater, Big State University School of Business. Acme is considering adding the dean of BSU's business school to the board of directors. Would the donations to the university cause a problem under the NYSE independence rules?

The NYSE position is that contributions to tax-exempt organizations, such as universities, generally are not considered "payments" for purposes of the independence rules. Accordingly, Acme's donations to BSU would not preclude a finding that the dean is independent. If the contributions exceed the greater of $1 million, or 2 percent of the tax-exempt organization's consolidated gross revenues, however, they must be disclosed in the company's annual proxy statement or Form 10-K. In addition, while such payments are not a per se bar to a finding of independence, the NYSE reminds listed company boards "of their obligations to consider the materiality of any such relationship in accordance with Section 303A.02(a)."

The NASDAQ and AMEX rules are substantially similar, although the dollar thresholds are lower and the freeze periods are shorter. The NASDAQ rule provides that:

"Independent director" means a person other than an officer or employee of the company or its subsidiaries or any other individual having a relationship which, in the opinion of the company's board of directors, would interfere with the exercise of independent judgment in carrying out the responsibilities of a director.

The NASDAQ holds board members appointed to the company's audit committee to a particularly high standard of independence. Audit committee members must not receive, directly or indirectly, any consulting, advisory, or other compensatory fee from the company or any of its subsidiaries. Audit committee members also must not have participated in the preparation of the company's financial statements at any time during the past three years.

FAMILY MEMBERS

The NYSE defines "immediate family member" as including "a person's spouse, parents, children, siblings, mothers and fathers-in-law, sons and daughters-in-law, brothers and sisters-in-law, and anyone (other than domestic employees) who shares such person's home." Note that the last clause would include both heterosexual and same-sex couples living together as domestic partners.

The Rationale for Director Independence

Does this mass of new rules make sense? In theory, independent directors are well suited to performing all of the board of directors' basic functions. With respect to the board's policy-making role, complex business decisions often require knowledge in such arcane areas as accounting, finance, management, and law. Including outsiders on the board who either are experts in such fields or have access to credible experts thus can improve the decision-making process. Diverse boards with lots of outsiders likely contain more specialists, and therefore should get greater benefits from specialization. On the other hand, because those specialists must be independent of management, the rules mandating director independence can have a negative impact on one of the board's other functions, namely, providing access to a network of contacts that may be useful in gathering resources and/or obtaining business.

At the very least, an outsider's perspective provides alternative viewpoints. In his 1972 book *Victims of Groupthink*, Irving Janis explained that groups of people who work together over an extended period of time often come to value consensus more greatly than they do a realistic appraisal of alternatives. Such groups strive for unanimity even at the expense of quality decision making. Unfortunately, in such groups, the desire to maintain social cohesion trumps the exercise of critical judgment. Adverse consequences of groupthink thus include not examining alternatives, being selective in gathering information, and failing to be either self-critical or evaluative of others.

One of the most famous examples of groupthink in business was RJR Tobacco's effort during the 1970s and early 1980s to develop a smokeless cigarette. Top management became preoccupied with the project, sinking over half-a-billion dollars into it. When the board of directors was finally informed of the project, many directors were infuriated by management's failure to consult with them. Their anger was wholly justified, because the smokeless cigarette flopped. Those managers responsible for the project resigned from the company to avoid being fired. The problem was that the managers in charge of the project had developed groupthink. Nobody in the team was willing to stand up and point out the many problems with the project. Only when outsiders on the board brought to bear their alternative perspective did the company finally wake up and stop shoveling money into this bottomless pit.

Having said all that, however, there's no guarantee an independent board will make better decisions than a board dominated by insiders. After all, a full-time senior manager has significant informational advantages over outsiders who devote but a small portion of their time and effort to the firm. At a minimum, the presence of outsiders on the board increases decision-making costs simply because the process takes longer. Outsiders by definition need more information and are likely to take longer to persuade than are insiders. More subtly, and perhaps more importantly, long-term employees make significant investments in firm-specific human capital. Any employee who advances to senior management levels necessarily invests considerable time and effort in learning how to do his job more effectively. Much of this knowledge will be specific to the firm for which he works. For example, a manager likely develops firm-specific information when other firms do not do comparable work or his firm has a unique corporate culture. In either case, the longer he works for the firm, the more firm-specific his human capital becomes. Such an employee is likely to make better decisions for the firm than an outsider, even assuming equal levels of information relating to the decision at hand. The insider can put the decision in a broader context, seeing the relationships and connections it has to the firm as whole.

Watching the Watchers

A similar analysis applies to the role of independent directors in carrying out the board's other main function, monitoring management. Let's start with a review of the board's management oversight role.

Why do companies have a board of directors at the top of the corporate hierarchy rather than a single autocratic leader? An important part of the answer to that question lies in the old Roman aphorism—*Quis custodiet ipsos custodes?*—Who watches the watchers?

All members of the corporate hierarchy have incentives to pursue their own self-interest rather than the interests of the shareholders. Sometimes the executive will just be tempted to shirk—to pursue leisure rather than working hard—but sometimes the temptation will be to cheat—to self-deal.

THE ECONOMICS OF SHIRKING AND CHEATING

Economists use the phrase *agency costs* when talking about the risk that employees will shirk or cheat. In economics lingo, a sole proprietor with no employees—that is, agents—will internalize all costs of shirking, because the proprietor's optimal tradeoff between labor and leisure is, by definition, the same as the firm's optimal tradeoff. In everyday language, if you own a business, you'll decide whether you'd rather make an extra buck by staying open longer or go home to watch *American Idol*. You'll make the tradeoff between work and leisure that makes you happiest.

Agents of a firm, however, do not internalize all of the costs of shirking: the principal reaps part of the value of hard work by the agent, but the agent receives all of the value of shirking. If I'm making ten dollars an hour, I'll make eighty dollars per day no matter how hard I work, so I'll be tempted to work just hard enough to keep you from firing me. I'll enjoy goofing when I'm supposed to be working, maybe by surfing the Internet, while you make less money, which is what economists call shirking.

Accordingly, an essential economic function of management is monitoring employees—management meters the marginal productivity of each employee and then takes steps to reduce shirking.

Accordingly, corporate employees and managers need to be monitored. Somebody needs to watch their performance to make sure they aren't shirking or cheating. But who watches the watcher?

In his wonderful children's book, *Did I Ever Tell You How Lucky You Are?*, Dr. Seuss told a story that nicely illustrates the problem. The story is about the town of Hawtch-Hawtch, whose principal industry is a bee. The townspeople hire a Bee-Watcher to watch the bee, because "[a] bee that is watched will work harder, you see." Unfortunately, the bee didn't work very hard. The townspeople concluded that this was the fault of the Bee-Watcher, so they decided to hire a Bee-Watcher-Watcher. But the latter also failed. So a Bee-Watcher-Watcher-Watcher was hired. Things progressed as one might expect, with the upshot being that soon all of Hawtch-Hawtch was out in the field watching one another.

Economists Armen Alchian and Harold Demsetz famously solved this dilemma by requiring that the ultimate monitor— the last Hawtch-Hawtcher in line—be given whatever profit is left over after everybody else gets paid. This so-called residual claim encourages the ultimate monitor to work hard, to promote the most efficient use of equipment and personnel, and to reduce shirking because his take-home earnings depend on how good a job he does of monitoring the firm's other workers. The better he watches, the more he makes.

Unfortunately, Alchian and Demsetz's otherwise quite useful model has limited application to the public corporation. Although common stockholders are the corporation's residual claimants, they also are the corporate constituency perhaps least able meaningfully to monitor management behavior.

Consequently, corporate law and governance must provide alternatives to shareholder monitoring. One of these alternatives is using a committee—the board—rather than an individual as the final monitor. Where an individual autocrat would have substantial freedom to shirk or self-deal, the internal dynamics of group governance constrain self-dealing and shirking by individual group members and even by the group as a whole. Within a group, mutual monitoring and peer pressure provide a coercive backstop for a set of interpersonal relationships founded on trust and other social norms.

Vesting the ultimate decision-making power in a group—the board—is therefore a potentially powerful solution to the problem of who watches the watchers. It creates a set of high-powered incentives for board members to comply with group standards for both effort and cooperation, and thus to be effective monitors of management.

Insiders or Outsiders: Who Makes the Best Monitors?

In theory, outside directors ought to be more effective monitors of management than insiders. Suppose you had a three-person board consisting of the CEO, the CFO, and the general counsel. Would the latter two really risk annoying their boss by telling the CEO he's doing a lousy job? If the board consisted of outsiders who aren't beholden to the CEO, they should be more likely to speak out or even fire an underperforming CEO.

If independent directors effectively monitor management, however, there should be an identifiable correlation between the presence of outsiders on the board and firm performance. Unfortunately, the considerable amount of empirical research by economists and management experts is, at best, mixed. Some studies find that shareholder wealth increases when management appoints independent directors. Some likewise find that boards consisting mainly of independent directors were more likely to base the decision to remove a CEO on poor performance, as well as being more likely to remove an underperforming CEO, than were insider-dominated boards.

Other studies, however, found that board composition had no effect on profitability. Indeed, some studies have found a positive correlation between the presence of insiders on board finance and investment committees and firm performance, which is directly counter to conventional wisdom.

In sum, there is no convincing evidence that firms with a majority of independent directors outperform other firms. To the contrary, there is some evidence that a moderate number of insiders on the board correlates with higher performance.

If independent directors are not effective monitors of senior management, why not? One obvious answer is that shirking is an endemic problem. Monitoring the performance of the firm's officers and employees is hard, time-consuming work. Moreover, most outside directors have full-time employment elsewhere, which commands the bulk of their attention and provides the bulk of their pecuniary and psychic income. Independent directors therefore may prefer leisure or working on their primary vocation to monitoring management. As Adam Smith observed over two centuries ago,

> The directors of [joint stock] companies, however, being the managers rather of other people's money than of their own, it cannot well be expected, that they should watch over it with the same anxious vigilance with which the partners in a private co-partnership frequently watch over their own. Like the stewards of a rich man, they are apt to consider attention to small matters as not for their master's honour, and very easily give themselves a dispensation from having it. Negligence and profusion, therefore, must always prevail, more or less, in the management of the affairs of such a company.

Other factors impede an independent director from monitoring management, even if he wishes to do so. Board meetings are few and short. According to one survey, directors in large manufacturing companies average a total of fourteen board and committee meetings per year, with the average board meeting lasting only three hours. Moreover, outside directors are generally dependent upon management for information.

Finally, even when nominally independent directors are not actually biased in favor of the insiders, they often are at least predisposed to favor insiders. Outside directors tend to be corporate officers or retirees who share the same views and values as the insiders. A sense of "there but for the grace of God go I" therefore is said to be a likely response when the CEO or other top managers get in trouble.

To be sure, the potential for shirking and bias easily can be overstated. Not all directors are biased, and the annals of corporate law are replete with instances in which seemingly biased directors nevertheless did the right thing. Better still, independent directors have affirmative incentives actively to monitor management and to discipline poor managers. If the company fails on their watch, for example, the independent directors' reputations, and thus their future employability, is likely to suffer.

Yet, even so, recent history teaches that board independence is hardly a panacea. The head of Enron's audit committee, Robert Jaedicke, was a professor of accounting at Stanford University, someone you would expect to be very highly qualified for his job.

And we all know what happened at Enron.

The Costs of Independence

If the benefits of director independence remain uncertain, the costs are clear. Public corporations are finding it increasingly difficult to recruit and retain qualified independent directors. Relatively low pay, compensation in stock rather than cash, and increased time demands and liability exposure have all combined to render board service far less attractive than it once was.

As a result, companies are spending more money on head-hunters to find good outside directors. They are also having to pay outside directors considerably higher fees, as well as paying ever-increasing director and officer liability insurance premiums. Economists James Linck, Jeffry Netter, and Tina Yang recently published a study entitled *Effects and Unintended Consequences of the Sarbanes-Oxley Act on Corporate Boards*, in which they confirmed that Sarbanes-Oxley has a significant impact on corporate boards of directors:

> Director workload and risk increased: audit committees meet more than twice as often post SOX as they did pre SOX, and Director and Officer (D&O) insurance premiums more than doubled. SOX also had a dramatic effect on the makeup of the corporate director pool: more post-SOX directors are lawyers/consultants, financial experts and retired executives, and fewer are current executives.

Whether these changes are providing significant corporate governance benefits is debatable; what is not subject to debate is that they are proving quite costly and, worse yet, those costs are being felt disproportionately by smaller public corporations.

> These changes drove a large increase in the cost of the board, particularly for small firms. For example, small firms paid $3.19 in director fees per $1,000 of net sales in 2004, which is $0.84

more than they paid in 2001 and $1.21 more than in 1998. In contrast, large firms paid $0.32 in director fees per $1,000 of net sales in 2004, seven cents more than they paid in 2001 and ten cents more than in 1998.

You can read their study at *http://papers.ssrn.com/sol3/papers .cfm?abstract_id=902665.*

One Size Doesn't Fit All

"One size fits all" is one of the great lies of our time, perhaps exceeded only by "the check is in the mail." This is true not only of hats and clothes, but also of corporate governance rules.

You often hear lawyers talk about standards and rules. The difference between the two is subtle but important. A speed limit is a good example of a rule: It sets out a bright line between what is lawful and what is not. The prohibition of driving negligently is a good example of a standard: It says that you should use reasonable care while driving, which leaves a lot of room for a judge or jury to evaluate your conduct based on the specific circumstances.

Business people often tend to like rules, because they provide greater certainty and predictability. The disadvantage of rules is that they typically are one-size-fits-all, which often isn't the case. What works for some companies may not work for others.

Whether a company ought to have a majority of independent directors is a good example of this phenomenon. A variety of forces work together to constrain management's incentive to shirk: the capital and product markets within which the firm functions, the internal and external markets for managerial services, the market for corporate control, incentive compensation systems, auditing by outside accountants, and others. The importance of the independent directors' monitoring role in a given firm depends in large measure on the extent to which these other forces are allowed to function. For example, managers of a firm with strong takeover defenses are less subject to the constraining influence of the market for corporate control than are those of a firm with no takeover defenses. The former needs a strong independent board more than the latter does. But SOX and the stock exchange listing requirements nevertheless locked almost all public corporations into a one-size-fits-all rule.

The proposition that one-size-fits-all rules like this one are a bad idea is confirmed by a recent research paper by two London School of Economics scholars, Sridhar R. Arcot and Valentina Giulia Bruno. (You can read their paper at *http://papers.ssrn.com/sol3/papers.cfm?abstract_id=887947.*) They explained that:

> We identify well-governed companies by accounting for heterogeneity in their governance choices by using a unique dataset. We find that companies that depart from governance best practice because of genuine circumstances outperform all others and cannot be considered badly governed. On the contrary, we find that mechanical adherence to best practice does not always lead to superior performance. We thus argue that flexibility in corporate governance regulation plays a crucial role, because companies are not homogenous entities.

Optimal Board Size

There's a very famous 1913 industrial psychology study that confirms the old adage "too many cooks spoil the broth." The researcher measured how hard subjects pulled on a rope. Members of two-person teams pulled to 93 percent of their individual capacity, members of trios pulled to only 85 percent, and members of groups of eight pulled to only 49 percent of capacity. The researcher named the phenomenon "social loafing." It's attributable partially to the difficulty of coordinating group effort as group size increases. Social loafing is also attributable, however, to the difficulty of motivating members of a group where identification and/or measurement of individual productivity is difficult—in other words, where the group functions as a team.

Although the social loafing phenomenon suggests that smaller boards probably are more effective, there are considerations cutting in the other direction. For example, larger boards may facilitate the board's resource-gathering function. Having more directors usually translates into more interlocking relationships with other organizations that may be useful in providing resources, such as customers, clients, credit, and supplies. Board interlocks may be especially helpful with respect to formation of strategic alliances. Larger boards with diverse interlocks are also likely to include a greater number of specialists—such as investment bankers or attorneys. Complex business decisions require knowledge in such areas as accounting, finance, management, and law. Providing access to such knowledge can be seen as part of the board's resource-gathering function. Board members may either possess such knowledge themselves or have access to credible external sources who do. Larger, more diverse boards likely contain more specialists, and therefore should get the benefit of specialization.

So is there an optimal board size? This is yet another situation in which one size likely does not fit all, but corporate governance experts generally agree that seven to nine members is the right size for most boards.

6

Board Committees and Proper Corporate Governance

Virtually all states allow the board to establish committees to which some board powers may be delegated, although a number do so only on an opt-in basis pursuant to which committee formation must be authorized by the articles of incorporation or bylaws. Section 141(c)(2) of the Delaware General Corporation Law, for example, provides that the board may set up one or more committees consisting of one or more members. The jurisdiction and powers of the committee must be specified either in the bylaws or in the board resolution creating the committee. All of the powers and authority of the board may be delegated to such committees, except that board committees are barred from acting on matters requiring shareholder approval or changes to the bylaws.

The NYSE Listed Company Manual mandates the establishment of three committees: a nominating and corporate governance committee (§ 303A.04), a compensation committee (§ 303A.05), and an audit committee (§ 303A.06). NASDAQ only requires establishment of an audit committee (as we'll see below, SOX required all the stock exchanges to adopt a mandatory audit committee rule).

The continuing proliferation of board committees is one reason boards are getting bigger. For a long time, there had been a trend toward smaller boards, with seven members having become typical. Most observers praised this trend, because smaller boards tend to work more effectively. With the additional required committees and all the additional duties being piled on committee members by SOX and the stock exchange requirements, however, the trend has reversed and boards are getting bigger again. Apparently, extra bodies are needed so that no one director ends up being overloaded with committee assignments and homework. Because size matters, the result may be less effective decision making by the board as a whole.

The Nominating and Corporate Governance Committee

NYSE Listed Company Manual § 303A.04 requires that listed companies set up "a nominating/corporate governance committee composed entirely of independent directors." The committee must have a written charter specifying how it will go about identifying candidates for board membership and selecting those candidates to be nominated. The committee should have sole power to select headhunters and negotiate their fees.

NASDAQ gives companies an alternative. Under Marketplace Rule 4350(c), new directors must be nominated either by a majority of the independent directors or a nominating committee comprised solely of independent directors.

The nominating power is vitally important. Board-of-director elections usually look a lot like old Soviet elections—there is only one slate of candidates and the authorities know how each voter voted. Absent the very unusual case of a proxy contest, in which a dissenting shareholder puts forward an alternative slate of director candidates, the slate nominated by the outgoing board of directors will be re-elected by default.

Corporate reformers long complained that boards simply rubberstamped the CEOs choices. In theory, having a separate committee of independent directors who are in charge of the nomination process should weaken the CEO's grip on power.

EXEMPTION FOR CONTROLLED COMPANIES

Both the NYSE and NASDAQ exempt companies in which a shareholder or group of shareholders acting together control 50 percent or more of the voting power of the company's stock from the nominating committee requirement.

There is some evidence to support this theory. Business school professors James Westphal and Edward Zajac demonstrated that as board power increases relative to the CEO—measured by such factors as the percentage of insiders and whether the CEO also served as chairman—newly appointed directors become more demographically similar to the board. In other words, instead of replicating the CEO and staffing the board with his cronies, independent directors controlling the nomination process replicate themselves and staff the board with their own cronies. Whether that's a good thing remains to be seen.

In addition to nominating director candidates, many companies assign responsibility for selecting new CEOs to the nominating committee. In cooperation with the compensation committee, the nominating committee may take the lead in negotiating the terms of a newly appointed CEO's employment agreement. Finally, the nominating committee may be tasked with setting director compensation, although many firms assign that job to the compensation committee.

Note that the NYSE listing requirement includes "corporate governance" as part of the nominating committee's job.

This aspect of the committee's duties remains relatively poorly defined. In general, however, the intent seems to be that the nominating committee should serve as the board of directors' principal point of contact with shareholders. As a practical matter, one common task given this committee is assigning directors to other board committees (typically subject to approval by the entire board).

An Overview of Proxy Voting

Most shareholders attend neither the corporation's annual meeting nor any special meetings. Instead, they are represented—and vote—by proxy. It's the corporate law equivalent of absentee balloting.

Shareholders send in a card (called a proxy card) on which they have marked their vote. The card authorizes a proxy agent to vote the shareholder's stock as directed on the card. The proxy card may specify how the shares are to be voted or may simply give the proxy agent discretion to decide how the shares are to be voted.

Under SEC Rule 14a-3, the incumbent board of directors' first step in soliciting proxies must be the distribution to shareholders of the firm's annual report. The annual report contains detailed financial statements and a discussion by management of the firm's business. It gives shareholders up-to-date information about what the firm is doing and a basis on which to assess how well management is performing.

Once the annual report is in the shareholders' hands, the proxy solicitation process can begin. The solicitor's goal is to get the shareholder to sign and date a proxy card, voting his shares in the manner the solicitor desires.

Along with the proxy card, the SEC requires that the solicitor provide solicited shareholders with a proxy statement containing mandated disclosures relating to the matters on the agenda.

The cover page of the proxy statement typically includes the state law–required notice of where and when the meeting is to be held, and will also state what issues are to be decided at the meeting. A proxy statement relating to an annual meeting, at which directors are elected, will typically open with biographical information about the candidates. The proxy statement will also include disclosures about board-of-director committees, board and executive compensation, relationships between the firm and its directors and senior officers, and a description of any other matters to come before the shareholders.

In the usual case, only the incumbent board of directors solicits proxies and the board's recommendations usually get overwhelming support from the shareholders. Occasionally, however, an independent shareholder (often called an insurgent) may solicit proxies in opposition to management. Usually the insurgent is putting forward a slate of directors as an alternative to the slate proposed by management. Rarely, the insurgent may solicit proxies in opposition to some proposal made by management. In either case, the process is doubled. Both sides independently prepare proxy cards and proxy statements that are separately sent to the shareholders.

SEC Disclosure Requirements and the Nominating Committee

Under SEC rules adopted in 2004, all reporting companies (whether or not they are NYSE- or NASDAQ-listed) must make disclosures in the annual proxy statement relating to the director nomination process. In particular, companies must disclose:

- Whether the company has established a standing nominating committee and, if not, the reasons why it did not do so
- Whether the members of the committee are independent

- Whether the nominating committee has adopted a written charter and, if so, how investors can obtain a copy (typically, from the corporate Web site)
- Whether the company has set up a process for shareholders to recommend prospective director nominees and, if so, how shareholders go about submitting such recommendations
- What minimum qualifications, if any, have been established for someone to serve as a director
- What procedures the committee uses to select nominees
- Whether the committee uses a paid headhunter
- Whether any person nominated to serve as a director was recommended by a shareholder, an outside director, the CEO, another executive officer, or a third-party search firm
- Whether a shareholder who has controlled more than 5 percent of the company's voting common stock for at least one year made any nominations and, if so, whether the committee chose to nominate such individual(s)

For a good example of how these disclosures work in practice, check out the Disney Company's 2006 proxy statement (available at *http://corporate.disney.go.com/investors/proxy/proxy_2006 .pdf*). Although the required disclosures are spread out across several sections of the proxy statement, a total of about three pages of double-column text was required to comply with just the SEC disclosure rules governing director nominations.

The SEC's Effort to Empower Shareholders to Nominate Directors

In 2003, the SEC proposed a dramatic shakeup in the process by which corporate directors are elected. At present, the director nomination machinery is under the control of the incumbent board of directors. When it is time to elect directors, the incumbent board nominates a slate, which it puts forward on the company's proxy statement.

There is no mechanism for a shareholder to put a nominee on the ballot. Instead, a shareholder who wishes to nominate directors is obliged to incur the considerable expense of conducting a proxy contest to elect a slate in opposition to that put forward by the incumbents.

If adopted, proposed new Rule 14a-11 would permit shareholders, upon the occurrence of certain specified events and subject to various restrictions, to have their nominees placed on the company's proxy statement and ballot. A shareholder-nominated director thus could be elected to the board in a fashion quite similar to the way shareholder-sponsored proposals are now put to a shareholder vote.

As proposed, Rule 14a-11 contemplated a two-step process stretching over two election cycles. Under the rule, a shareholder may place his or her nominee on the corporation's proxy card and statement if one of two triggering events occurs:

1. A shareholder proposal is made under Rule 14a-8 to authorize shareholder nominations, which is approved by the holders of a majority of the outstanding shares at a meeting of the shareholders; or
2. Shareholders representing at least 35 percent of the votes withhold authority on their proxy cards for their shares to be voted in favor of any director nominated by the incumbent board of directors.

At the next annual meeting of the shareholders at which directors are elected, shareholder nominees would be included in the company's proxy statement and ballot.

SEC Rule 14a-8 provides a limited right for a shareholder to put an issue before the other shareholders for a vote, with the question placed on the proxy card ballot and a supporting statement included in the company's proxy statement.

Thus, the chief advantage of the shareholder proposal rule, from the perspective of the proponent, is that it is cheap. The proponent need not pay any of the printing and mailing costs, all of which must be paid by the corporation, or otherwise comply with the expensive panoply of regulatory requirements.

SHAREHOLDER PROPOSALS

Corporate law essentially treats the company's proxy card and proxy statement as belonging to the incumbent board of directors. The board decides what issues will be put to a shareholder vote—in practice, of course, this is done in consultation with the CEO and general counsel—and, subject to SEC disclosure rules, what to say in the proxy statement. Shareholders have no state-law right to put something on the ballot or to include any material in the proxy statement.

Not all shareholder proposals must be included in the proxy statement. Rule 14a-8 lays out various eligibility requirements, which a shareholder must satisfy in order to be eligible to use the rule. The rule also lays out various procedural hurdles the shareholder must clear. Finally, the rule identifies a number of substantive bases for excluding a proposal.

For more information, check out this Web site: *www.share holderproposals.com.*

Not all shareholders would be entitled to make use of the nomination process. Only shareholders satisfying four criteria would have access to the company's proxy materials; namely, a shareholder or group of shareholders who: (1) beneficially own more than 5 percent of the company's voting stock and have held the requisite number of shares continuously for at least two years as of the date of the nomination; (2) state an intent to continue owning the requisite number of securities through the date of the relevant shareholders meeting; (3) are eligible to report their holdings on Schedule 13G, rather than Schedule 13D; and (4) have filed a Schedule 13G before their nomination is submitted to the corporation. Because the eligibility requirements for use of Schedule 13G include a disclaimer of intent to seek control of the corporation, proposed Rule 14a-11 supposedly could not become a tool for corporate acquisitions.

Data reported in the SEC's proposing release suggest that 42 percent of registered issuers already had at least one shareholder who would be able to make use of Rule 14a-11, although one must wonder how many of those companies are already de facto controlled by that shareholder. If most are, the key issue with respect to how often Rule 14a-11 would be used in practice is not how many corporations already have one or more large shareholders, but rather how many have a handful of institutional investors, each owning perhaps 1 percent of the company's shares, who would band together to form the requisite group.

The number of nominees who could be put forward by a qualifying shareholder depends on the number of board positions. A company whose board consists of eight or fewer directors would be required to include one security holder nominee. A company with a board of directors having more than eight but fewer than twenty members would be obliged to include two shareholder nominees. A company with twenty or more board members would be obliged to allow three nominees to be included on the proxy materials. Where the terms of the board members are staggered, the relevant consideration is the size of the board as a whole rather than the size of the class to be elected in that year.

In order for an individual to be eligible to be nominated, that individual must satisfy the applicable stock exchange definition of independence from the company. To avoid the use of surrogate director nominees by the incumbents, there can be no agreement between the nominee or nominating group and the company. Perhaps more surprising, however, the proposal also contemplates that the nominee will satisfy a number of independence criteria (e.g., no family or employment relationships) vis-à-vis the nominating shareholder or group. The SEC clearly was concerned that the proposal might be used to put forward special-interest directors who would not represent the shareholders as a whole but only the narrow interests of those who nominated them.

In addition to the two triggering events incorporated into the rule as proposed, the SEC solicited comments on a possible third triggering event with three criteria:

[A] A security holder proposal submitted pursuant to Exchange Act Rule 14a-8, other than a direct access security holder proposal, was submitted for a vote of security holders at an annual meeting by a security holder or group of security holders that held more than 1% of the company's securities entitled to vote on the proposal for one year and provided evidence of such holdings to the company;

[B] The security holder proposal received more than 50% of the votes cast on that proposal; and

[C] The board of directors of the company failed to implement the proposal by the 120th day prior to the date that the company mailed its proxy materials for the [subsequent] annual meeting.

As the SEC acknowledged, adopting this trigger would invite time-consuming disputes on such minutiae as whether the board failed to implement the proposal. There was an even more fundamental flaw with this third trigger, however.

State corporate law provides that the key player in the statutory decision-making structure is the corporation's board of directors. As the Delaware code puts it, the corporation's business and affairs "shall be managed by or under the direction of a board of directors." Accordingly, the vast majority of corporate decisions are made by the board of directors alone (or by managers acting under delegated authority). Shareholders essentially have no power to initiate corporate action and, moreover, are entitled to approve or disapprove only a very few board actions. The statutory decision-making model thus is one in which the board acts and shareholders, at most, react.

The third proposed trigger would have shifted that balance of power in favor of the shareholders. At present, the vast majority of shareholder proposals under SEC Rule 14a-8 must be phrased as recommendations rather than as directives to the board. If a precatory proposal passes but the board of directors decides after due deliberation not to accept the shareholders' recommendation, the board's decision currently is protected by the business judgment rule. (In legal terms, "precatory" refers to a suggestion that does not have the force of a legal demand.) Hence, the board's power of direction is insulated from being trumped by the shareholders. To be sure, the proposed trigger would not mandate that boards implement precatory proposals. It would, however, ratchet up the pressure on boards to accede to shareholder proposals even when the board in the exercise of its business judgment believes the proposal to be unwise. In order to avoid a shareholder nomination contest, the board therefore might implement a proposal it deems unsound.

The SEC proposal made little policy sense. The impact of a shareholder right to elect board members on the effectiveness of the board's decision-making processes will be analogous to that of cumulative voting. Granted, some firms benefit from the presence of skeptical outsider viewpoints. It is well accepted, however, that cumulative voting tends to promote adversarial relations between the majority and the minority representative. That cumulative voting results in personal conflict rather than cognitive conflict thus leaves one doubtful as to whether firms actually benefit from minority representation.

As of this writing, the SEC has neither adopted nor withdrawn the proposed rule. At this point, over three years hence, it seems unlikely that the SEC will go forward. At many companies, however, shareholders are demanding changes to the bylaws or articles of incorporation that would create similar mechanisms for shareholders to put nominees on the company's proxy statement. The SEC has flip-flopped on whether shareholders can use the Rule 14a-8 shareholder proposal process to put such bylaw amendments on the ballot. At present, the SEC takes the position that Rule 14a-8(i)(8), which forbids shareholders from putting forward proposals relating to election of directors, bars bylaw amendments of this type. Accordingly, at some companies, militant shareholders have initiated proxy contests seeking to amend the bylaws.

Changing the Vote Required

One of the curiosities of the corporate electoral system is that it does not actually provide for a straight up or down, for or against, vote for directors. Instead, under SEC Rule 14a-4(b), the company must give shareholders three options on the proxy card: vote for all of the nominees for director, withhold support for all of them, or withhold support from specified directors by striking out their names.

Withholding support is not the same as a vote against, absent a contested election. Delaware General Corporation

Law § 216(3) provides: "Directors shall be elected by a plurality of the votes of the shares present in person or represented by proxy at the meeting and entitled to vote on the election of directors." The Comments to Model Business Corporation Act § 7.28(a), which also uses a "plurality" standard, explains that: "A 'plurality' means that the individuals with the largest number of votes are elected as directors up to the maximum number of directors to be chosen at the election."

Suppose, for example, that the company has five vacancies and there are exactly five candidates. The holders of a majority of the company's voting shares of stock withhold authority to vote for Director Dan. Indeed, only a single shareholder who owned just one share (out of 100 million outstanding shares) voted for Dan. Under the plurality voting system, Dan is elected.

Institutional investors increasingly withhold their votes from selected director candidates at companies they believe are underperforming. The best known example of this was the 2004 campaign by a group of Disney shareholders against then-CEO and board chairman Michael Eisner. Holders of over one-third of Disney's shares withheld their votes from Eisner. Although he won re-election, the embarrassment of having such a strong showing of shareholder dissatisfaction contributed to Eisner's subsequent decision to step down.

In order to put real teeth into a withhold vote campaign, institutional investors have been vigorously and successfully lobbying state legislatures to change the plurality rule to a majority vote requirement. Thanks to recently approved amendments, both the Model Business Corporation Act (in force in over thirty-five states) and the Delaware General Corporation Law now permit majority voting for directors. Under both, the default rule remains the traditional plurality, but companies may adopt majority voting by putting it into the bylaws or articles of incorporation.

There is no consensus best practice for dealing with the majority versus plurality vote question. With the recent state law changes in hand, however, institutional investors are campaigning hard for companies to adopt some form of majority vote system.

A company considering doing so needs to evaluate a number of issues:

- Would a majority vote requirement apply to both contested and uncontested elections? Typically, it applies only in uncontested votes (i.e., where the number of candidates equals the number of vacancies to be filled).
- If one or more directors do not receive the requisite vote, how will you fill the resulting vacancies? Will the elected board members choose replacements or will there have to be a special shareholder vote?
- Do any potential director candidates have employment agreements that would be affected by failure to be elected? Many CEOs, for example, have employment agreements providing that the agreement will be terminated if they are not elected to the board and also providing for substantial severance payments in that event.
- Many corporate contracts have provisions that terminate the agreement or impose other sanctions in the event there is a change in control of the company. Would those agreements trigger if a substantial number of directors were not elected?
- How will abstentions be handled?

The default rule under the Model Business Corporation Act § 7.25(c) is that "action on a matter [other than election of directors] is approved if the votes cast . . . favoring the action exceed the votes cast opposing the action." In contrast, Delaware

General Corporation Law § 216 states that "the affirmative vote of the majority of shares present in person or represented by proxy at the meeting and entitled to vote on the subject matter shall be the act of the stockholders." The distinction between the two formulations is subtle but significant. Suppose there are 1,000 shares entitled to vote, 800 of which are represented at the meeting either in person or by proxy, and they are voted as follows: in Favor, 399; Opposed, 398; Abstain, 3. Under the Model Act, the motion carries, as more shares voted in favor of the motion than against it. Under the Delaware statute, however, a majority of the shares present at the meeting—in this case, 401—must be voted in favor of the motion for it to carry, and this motion therefore fails. In effect, Delaware treats abstentions as no votes, while the Model Act ignores them. My advice would be for a company to use the Model Act approach in drafting a majority vote provision.

The majority vote movement is one of the shareholder activists' greatest successes. It is going to be around for a while. Companies therefore need to start facing these questions. Now.

Board Reform and Shareholder Activism

In the wake of the shareholder revolt at Disney and the other developments discussed in the sections above, big institutional investors are feeling their oats. The American Federation of State, County, and Municipal Employees (AFSCME) and other union pension funds sponsored almost half the shareholder proposals on proxy statements during the latest annual meeting cycle. They were also among the leading advocates of the SEC's proposal to let shareholders nominate directors. It was CalPERS—the big California public employee pension fund—that made perhaps the biggest splash by announcing in 2004 that it would oppose re-election of some or all of the directors of over 2,700 companies.

The "perfect storm" metaphor is overused to the point of becoming a cliché, but how else can one describe the Disney fight? We saw a combination of long-term performance woes, a widely disliked and autocratic CEO, a hostile takeover bid in the offing, and a crew of dissident ex-directors—including a member of the founding family—leading a shareholder revolt. The big question was whether activist shareholders could catch the same lightning in a more routine bottle.

A 1998 survey by Stanford law professor Bernard Black found relatively little evidence that shareholder activism matters in corporate governance except perhaps at the very margins. Most institutional investors historically spent only trifling amounts on corporate governance activism. Most devote little effort to monitoring management; on the contrary, they typically disclaim the ability or desire to decide company-specific policy questions. They rarely conduct proxy solicitations or put forward shareholder proposals. They tend not to try to elect representatives to boards of directors. They rarely coordinate their activities. (You can read Black's study here: *http://papers.ssrn .com/sol3/papers.cfm?abstract_id=45100*.)

Does the recent spurt of activism on the part of pension funds like CalPERS suggest a major shift in the behavior of institutional investors since 1998? It seems unlikely. The vast majority of institutional investors—like banks, insurers, mutual funds, and private pension funds—show little interest in corporate governance activism.

Instead, activism is principally the province of a very limited group of institutions. Almost exclusively, the activists are union and state employee pension funds. They are the ones using shareholder proposals to pressure management. They are the ones most likely to seek board representation. As AFSCME chairman Gerald McEntee told *Los Angeles Times* columnist James Flanigan: "We're not looking to take over the corporation, but to have a voice through one or two or three seats on the board."

One might reasonably wonder what a public employee union knows about running business corporations. Might they have another agenda for board representation?

The interests of large and small investors often differ. As management becomes more beholden to the interests of large shareholders, it may become less concerned with the welfare of smaller investors. If the large shareholders with the most influence are unions or state pensions, however, the problem is exacerbated.

The interests of unions as investors differ radically from those of ordinary investors. The pension fund of the union representing Safeway workers, for example, tried to oust directors who stood up to the union in collective bargaining negotiations. Union pension funds have used shareholder proposals to obtain employee benefits they couldn't get through bargaining (although the SEC usually doesn't allow these proposals onto the proxy statement). AFSCME's involvement is especially worrisome; the public sector employee union is highly politicized and seems especially likely to use its pension funds as a vehicle for advancing political/social goals unrelated to shareholder interests generally.

Public pension funds are even more likely to do so. Indeed, the *Los Angeles Times* reported that CalPERS' renewed activism was "fueled partly by the political ambitions of Phil Angelides, California's state treasurer and a CalPERS board member." Such abuse of public pension funds by incumbent politicians is unfair to their political opponents, other investors, and especially the retirees who depend on those funds. Studies have consistently shown that the greater the extent to which a public pension fund is subject to direct political control, the worse its investment returns.

More than half of Americans are now stock investors. Yet, only a select, self-appointed few have become activists. All too often, their activism is directed at selfish interests inconsistent with those of investors at large. It's long past time for the SEC and Congress to consider whether these investors need greater limits rather than greater powers.

The Compensation Committee

As the name suggests, the compensation committee reviews and approves (or recommends to the full board) the compensation of senior executives and generally oversees the corporation's compensation policies. Proponents of having a separate compensation committee deal with such matters, rather than the board as a whole, argue that inside directors, even if recused from considering their own compensation, cannot objectively evaluate the compensation of other senior executives in light of the close relationship between one executive's compensation and that of another.

NYSE and NASDAQ Requirements

Under NYSE Listed Company Manual § 303A.05, the board of directors of all listed companies must have a compensation committee. The committee must consist solely of independent directors. Only listed companies in which a shareholder or group of shareholders acting together own 50 percent or more of the stock are exempt from this requirement.

Jane is a director of Ajax Corporation. Jane is also the CFO of Zeus Corporation. Donna is Ajax's CLO (aka general counsel), a member of Zeus's board of directors, and a member of Zeus's compensation committee. Under the NYSE rule, because Donna is on Zeus's compensation committee, Jane cannot be deemed an independent director of Ajax. Donna can be deemed an independent director of Zeus, however, because the interlock rule runs in only one direction.

COMPENSATION COMMITTEE INTERLOCKS AND DIRECTOR INDEPENDENCE

The NYSE definition of *independent director* excludes the following: "The director or an immediate family member is, or has been within the last three years, employed as an executive officer of another company where any of the listed company's present executive officers at the same time serves or served on that company's compensation committee."

The NYSE also requires that the compensation committee adopt a written charter setting out the committee's purpose, responsibilities, and powers. At a minimum, the compensation committee must have power to:

(A) Set performance goals for the CEO to meet, evaluate the CEO's performance in light of those goals, and set the CEO's pay. If the board wishes, the compensation committee may simply recommend a pay figure for the CEO, on which all the independent directors would then act.

(B) Make recommendations to the board of directors with respect to the pay of other executive officers and any incentive or stock-based compensation plans that are subject to board approval.

(C) Produce a compensation committee report on executive officer compensation to be included in the listed company's annual proxy statement or annual report on Form 10-K.

It's become quite common for companies to get advice from consultants in setting executive pay. The NYSE expects that the charter will vest the power to hire, fire, and compensate such consultants in the compensation committee rather than the CEO.

The NASDAQ rule on compensation is similar to the NASDAQ rule on board nominations:

(A) Compensation of the chief executive officer of the company must be determined, or recommended to the Board for determination, either by: (i) a majority of the independent directors, or (ii) a compensation committee comprised solely of independent directors. The chief executive officer may not be present during voting or deliberations.

(B) Compensation of all other executive officers must be determined, or recommended to the Board for determination, either by: (i) a majority of the independent directors, or (ii) a compensation committee comprised solely of independent directors.

Again, a company that has a shareholder or group of shareholders acting together that own more than 50 percent of the company's equity securities is exempt from this requirement. NASDAQ also allows the company to appoint a single non-independent board member to the compensation committee (for a period of up to two years), so long as the company discloses why it believes doing so is in the company's interest.

Effective July 2006, the SEC began requiring a "Compensation Committee Report" in which the company states whether the compensation committee has discussed the Compensation Discussion and Analysis (CD&A) disclosures with management and whether the committee recommended that the CD&A be included in the company's annual Form 10-K and its proxy statement.

SEC Executive Compensation Disclosure Rules

The SEC requires all reporting companies to include fairly extensive executive compensation disclosures in the annual proxy statement. Those disclosures must include:

- The summary compensation table, which the SEC calls "the cornerstone," because it "provides, in a single location, a comprehensive overview of a company's executive pay practices." The table summarizes both the annual pay and deferred compensation of the company's CEO, CFO, and the three other most highly compensated executive officers. The figure below is the sample summary table provided by the SEC at *www.sec.gov.*
- The option grant and exercise tables, which report how many stock options were granted to and exercised by top executives.
- The deferred compensation plan tables, which disclose long-term incentive plan awards and pension funds.
- A summary of director fees and other director compensation.
- A report on any compensation committee interlocks and insider participation in compensation decisions.
- A report from the board's compensation committee on executive compensation, which explains how the committee goes about assessing executive performance and setting executive pay.

Sample Summary Compensation Table

Name and Principal Position (a)	Year (b)	Salary ($) (c)	Bonus ($) (d)	Stock Awards ($) (e)	Option Awards ($) (f)	Non-Equity Incentive Plan Compensation ($) (g)	Change in Pension Value and Nonqualified Deferred Compensation Earnings ($) (h)	All Other Compensation ($) (i)	Total ($) (j)
PEO[1]									
PFO[2]									
A									
B									
C									

Note: "PEO" refers to principal executive officer, and "PFO" to principal financial officer.

SEC RESOURCES

For a summary of SEC disclosure rules in this area, go to the SEC's Web site: *www.sec.gov/investor/pubs/execomp0803 .htm*. For the press release announcing the July 2006 changes, go to *www.sec.gov/news/press/2006/2006-123 .htm*.

In July 2006, the SEC adopted new disclosure rules supplementing the existing regime. The principal change is a new Compensation Discussion and Analysis (CD&A), which will have to be filed with the SEC and thus will be one of the disclosures subject to § 302 certification by the company's CEO and CFO. The CD&A is to be a narrative discussion, written in plain English rather than legalese.

One area of particular emphasis will be the CD&A's analysis of option-related information, "such as the reasons a company selects particular grant dates for awards or the methods a company uses to select the terms of awards, such as the exercise prices of stock options." The focus on disclosure relating to the timing of option grants is clearly intended to prevent either backdating or spring-loading options.

The CD&A disclosure will lead off the compensation section of the Form 10-K and proxy statement. It will be followed by three sections: (1) executive compensation paid in the last three years, (2) stock-based compensation (the option tables are incorporated into this section), and (3) retirement plans and other forms of deferred compensation (the deferred compensation tables are incorporated here).

Compensation Committee Best Practices

A report by former SEC Chairman Richard Breeden to the WorldCom board of directors, in which he made numerous recommendations for improving WorldCom's corporate governance, provides an overview of emerging best practices:

1. *Committee Membership:* Breeden recommended that the committee "consist of not less than three members, each of whom should be an independent director who possesses experience with compensation and human resources issues."

2. *Meeting Requirements:* The committee should meet not less than four times per year to evaluate the performance of the CEO and other top management. At least once a year, the committee should get a training session on how to evaluate executive performance and otherwise comply with its various duties.

3. *Compensation Consultants:* Any outside consultants should be hired and fired by the committee, which also should have sole power to set the consultant's pay.

4. *Turnover:* To prevent the committee members from getting too cozy with management, there should be regular turnover of the committee membership. In particular, the chair of the committee should rotate at least once every three years.

5. *Compensation Committee Compensation:* The pay of committee members should be high enough to encourage them to devote substantial effort to their duties. For WorldCom, Breeden recommended that committee members receive at least $35,000 per year and the chairman receive at least $50,000 per year.

6. *Oversight:* "At least twice each year the Compensation Committee should meet with the Director of Human Resources and the General Counsel to review (i) compliance with the Company's prohibitions against any related party transactions between directors or employees and their families and the Company or any of its affiliates; (ii) compliance with SEC proxy disclosure standards, and (iii) all employee complaints, disputes or issues regarding human resources or compensation issues."

To review Breeden's full report, which contains lots of useful information about emerging best practices in a number of areas, go to: *www.thedirectorscollege.com/images/downloads/ Breeden%20Report%20Restoring%20Trust.pdf.*

Does Management Have Too Much Power over Its Own Compensation?

Executive compensation has grown by leaps and bounds over the last two decades. By 2003, the average large-firm CEO made 500 times what the average worker made. In the aggregate, during the five-year period 1998–2002, compensation paid to the top five executives at 1,500 large public corporations totaled roughly $100 billion.

Yet, we live in an era in which many occupations carry such vast rewards. Lead actors routinely earn $20 million per film. The NBA's average salary is over $4 million per year. Top investment bankers can earn annual bonuses of $5 to $15 million. Unless one's objection is solely based on the size of executive compensation, perhaps for redistributionist reasons, critics of executive compensation must be able to distinguish corporate managers from these other highly paid occupations.

Among the many critics of current executive compensation practices, law professors Lucian Bebchuk and Jesse Fried contend that actors and sports stars bargain at arm's length with their employers, while managers essentially set their own compensation. As a result, they claim, even though managers are under a fiduciary duty to maximize shareholder wealth, executive compensation arrangements often fail to provide executives with proper incentives to do so and may even cause executive and shareholder interests to diverge. In other words, the executive compensation scandal is not the rapid growth of management pay in recent years, as too many glibly opine, but rather the failure of compensation schemes to award high pay only for top performance.

Bebchuk and Fried's analysis is premised on what they call "managerial power." They claim that "directors have been influenced by management, sympathetic to executives, insufficiently motivated to bargain over compensation, or simply ineffectual in overseeing compensation." As a result, executive pay has greatly exceeded the levels that would prevail if directors loyal to shareholder interests actually bargained with managers at arm's length.

Conventional wisdom says that the principal-agent problem is the central issue of corporate governance. Agents who shirk do not internalize all of the costs thereby created; the principal reaps part of the value of hard work by the agent, but the agent receives all of the value of shirking. Wherever a principal-agent problem exists, we thus expect to see a mixture of carrots and sticks designed to constrain shirking. The sticks include ex post sanctions, up to and including dismissal. The carrots include incentives that align the agent's interests with those of the principal.

In theory, executive compensation schemes that realign the interests of corporate managers with those of the shareholders could ameliorate the principal-agent problem. In practice, however, the most common forms of executive compensation fail to remedy the principal-agent problem. Indeed, some forms exacerbate the problem.

According to critics of current compensation practices, boards of directors—even those nominally independent of management—have strong incentives to acquiesce in executive compensation that pays managers rents (i.e., amounts in excess of the compensation management would receive if the board had bargained with them at arm's length). Among these are: Directors often are chosen de facto by the CEO. Once a director is on the board, pay and other incentives give the director a strong interest in being re-elected; in turn, due to the CEO's considerable influence over selection of the board slate, this gives directors an incentive to stay on the CEO's good side. Directors who work closely with top management develop feelings of loyalty and affection for those managers, as well as becoming inculcated with norms of collegiality and team spirit, which induce directors to "go along" with bloated pay packages. Finally, those directors who resist these incentives and seek to put shareholder interests first face a number of obstacles in both the law and practice of corporate governance.

The net effect of managerial power is that CEO pay packets are higher than would obtain under arm's length bargaining and less sensitive to performance. As a result, compensation of CEOs and other top managers has become a not insignificant chunk of corporate earnings. Yet, critics claim, much of that pay has been insensitive to the performance of those companies.

While critics like Bebchuk and Fried have gathered considerable evidence in support of their complaints, there is much competing evidence suggesting that executive compensation packages are designed to align managerial and shareholder interests. Consider, for example, the much-maligned practice of management perquisites. If managerial power has widespread traction as an explanation of compensation practices, one would assume that the evidence would show no correlation between the provision of perks and shareholder interests. In fact, however, the *Economist* recently reported on an interesting study of executive perks finding just the opposite:

> Raghuram Rajan, the IMF's chief economist, and Julie Wulf, of the Wharton School, looked at how more than 300 big companies dished out perks to their executives in 1986–99. It turns out that neither cash-rich, low-growth firms nor firms with weak governance shower their executives with unusually generous perks. The authors did, however, find evidence to support two competing explanations.
>
> First, firms in the sample with more hierarchical organizations lavished more perks on their executives than firms with flatter structures. Why? Perks are a cheap way to demonstrate status. Just as the armed forces ration medals, firms ration the distribution of conspicuous symbols of corporate status.
>
> Second, perks are a cheap way to boost executive productivity. Firms based in places where it takes a long time to commute are more likely to give the boss a chauffeured limousine. Firms located far from large airports are likelier to lay on a corporate jet.
>
> In other words, executive perks seem to be set with shareholder interests in mind, which is inconsistent with the possibility that managerial power offers a unified field theory of executive compensation.

This example is not intended as a comprehensive rebuttal of the critics' arguments, but rather to highlight the possibility that many executive compensation practices are at least as consistent with an arm's length bargaining model as the managerial power model.

In any case, many of the critics' principal complaints no longer have as much validity as they may once have had. As we've seen, in June 2002, the NYSE's board approved new listing standards that significantly enlarged the role and power of independent members of listed companies' boards of directors. NASDAQ and AMEX adopted similar changes. A number of the new listing standards speak directly to the critics' arguments.

Under the NYSE's new listing standards, for example, listed companies must create a compensation committee, comprised solely of independent directors, whose minimal duties include setting the CEO's compensation. The committee must adopt written charters specifying their roles, duties, and powers, which must at a minimum conform to the listing standard's detailed requirements. The committee now hires compensation consultants, a task previously left to management. To address the long-standing problem of director interlocks, in which the CEO of two companies would sit on each other's board of directors' compensation committee, and presumably scratch each other's backs, the new listing standards provide that a director may not be deemed independent if he is employed (or has been employed in the last five years) by a company in which an executive officer of the listed company serves as a member of the board of directors' compensation committee.

The NYSE's new standards also require that all listed corporations create a nominating and corporate governance committee comprised solely of independent directors. The new listing standards also substantially limit the CEO's ability financially to reward compliant directors. The new rules, for example, limit the amount of additional compensation directors may receive over and above their director fees. They also limit the amount of business allowed between the corporation and a business associated with one of its independent directors.

Finally, the NYSE's new stock exchange listing standards significantly tighten the definition of director independence. To be sure, the evidence as to the corporate governance value of director independence is mixed, at best. Yet, the new rules are only now taking effect. It may be too early to tell whether the new rules will make significant changes.

Should the law be changed to regulate executive compensation more closely? At this point, the best solution is likely that we should wait and see what happens with the recent reforms before rushing forward with more changes in the law.

The Audit Committee

The data contained in a corporation's financial statements is the market's best tool for evaluating how well a firm's managers perform. Because management prepares the financial statements, however, how can the market trust those statements to represent fairly and accurately the company's true financial picture? Would managers really tell the truth if it meant losing their jobs?

To ensure that the financial statements are accurate and complete, the SEC requires corporations to have those statements audited by an independent firm of certified public accountants. In order to prevent management and the outside auditor from getting too cozy with one another, it's long been good practice for the corporation's board of directors to have an audit committee. Ideally, the audit committee provides a forum for independent directors to discuss the firm's financial results outside of management's presence and ensures that the audited financial statements fairly and accurately represent the company's financial picture.

Enron, WorldCom, and the various other scandals of 2000–2002, especially those involving former Big Six accounting firm Arthur Andersen, demonstrated that there were serious problems with all of the key players: management, the outside auditor, and the board of directors and its audit committee. The wave of restated financials in 2001–2002 confirmed that there were basic, widespread problems with the financial disclosures provided by many companies. Congress, the SEC, and the stock exchanges struck back in various ways. In this section, we'll look at the important changes they made to the role and powers of the audit committee.

SOX Mandates Audit Committees

For decades, the NYSE required listed companies to have an audit committee consisting solely of independent directors. The committee had to have at least three members, all of whom were "financially literate." At least one committee member had to have expertise in accounting or financial management.

WHAT'S AN AUDIT COMMITTEE?

SOX defines the term *audit committee* as "a committee (or equivalent body) established by and amongst the board of directors of an issuer for the purpose of overseeing the accounting and financial reporting processes of the issuer and audits of the financial statements of the issuer."

When Sarbanes-Oxley was under consideration by Congress, a consensus quickly formed in favor of imposing a tougher version of the NYSE requirements on all public corporations. SOX § 301 therefore ordered the SEC to adopt rules requiring that the stock exchanges and NASDAQ adopt listing requirements mandating the creation by listed companies of audit committees satisfying the following specifications:

1. *Committee Responsibilities*: The audit committee is responsible for appointing, compensating, and supervising the company's outside auditor. The outside auditor "shall report directly to the audit committee." The committee also must resolve "disagreements between management and the auditor regarding financial reporting."

2. *Independence*: All members of the audit committee must be independent, which § 301 defines as precluding the committee member from being an "affiliated person" of the company and from accepting any "consulting, advisory, or other compensatory fee" from the company except for directors' fees.

3. *Whistle Blowers*: The audit committee must establish procedures for handling complaints about the way the company conducts its accounting, internal audit controls, and outside audits. The procedure must include a mechanism for "the confidential, anonymous submission by employees . . . of concerns regarding questionable accounting or auditing matters."

4. *Hiring Advisors*: In addition to empowering the audit committee to hire and pay the outside auditor, the company also must empower the committee to hire "independent counsel and other advisors, as it determines necessary to carry out its duties," with the outside advisor's fees paid by the company.

Rule 10A-3 is the principal SEC rule implementing § 301. (The text of the rule is available at *www.law.uc.edu/CCL/34ActRls/rule10A-03.html*.) One of its critical provisions is the definition of *affiliated person*, which includes persons who own more than 10 percent of the company's stock, company directors, and executive officers of the company. If the 10 percent-plus shareholder is a corporation, partnership, or limited liability company, any director who is an employee of such company, or an executive officer, partner, or managing member of such company, is also deemed an affiliated person.

INSIDE ADVISORS

Although the rules contemplate that boards and board committees may look to outside advisors, it's important to remember that the board properly may seek advice and information from in-house advisors, especially the CFO and general counsel. Although they may report to the CEO, the CFO and general counsel ultimately work for the board and have an obligation to provide unbiased advice and information. This is particularly true of the general counsel, because the general counsel has a lawyer-client relationship with the corporation, as represented by the board of directors, the legal ethics rules. Of course, in turn, the board has an obligation to protect the CFO and general counsel from retaliation by a CEO upset by their "going over my head."

The NYSE and NASDAQ Audit Committee Rules

SOX became law while the NYSE and NASDAQ were working up their own reforms to boards, which included planned changes to the audit committee. SOX § 301 and the SEC rules adopted to implement it thus had to be worked into the stock exchanges' plans. Given that § 301 told the SEC to tell the exchanges to fix the problem, subject to certain guidelines, however, it is the stock exchange listing requirements that provide the critical rules of the game for the post-SOX audit committee.

NYSE Listed Company Manual § 303A.06 says that each listed company must have an audit committee. Unlike the nominating and compensation committee requirements, even companies with a controlling shareholder must comply with the audit committee rules.

In § 303A.07, the NYSE sets out additional committee requirements:

- The committee must have at least three members. (Note that a growing number of firms are appointing as many as five individuals to the audit committee so as to help share the high workload imposed on this committee's members.)
- All committee members must be independent, both as defined in SOX § 301 and the NYSE Listed Company Manual.
- All committee members must be "financially literate" and at least one member "must have accounting or related financial management expertise." It's left up to the company's board of directors to decide what that means and whether the members qualify.
- The audit committee must have a written charter specifying its duties, role, and powers.

DO INDEPENDENT AUDIT COMMITTEES ADD VALUE?

Economists have studied whether having wholly independent audit committees improves company performance not only in the United States, but also in Australia and the United Kingdom. None of those studies found that having an independent audit committee added measurable value. Yale law professor Roberta Romano summarizes these studies at *http://papers .ssrn.com/sol3/papers.cfm?abstract_id=596101.*

- The committee is charged with oversight of "(1) the integrity of the listed company's financial statements, (2) the listed company's compliance with legal and regulatory requirements, (3) the independent auditor's qualifications and independence, and (4) the performance of the listed company's internal audit function and independent auditors."

- The committee must prepare an annual report on the audit process to be included in the company's annual proxy statement.

- The audit committee must establish procedures for receiving and dealing with complaints "regarding accounting, internal accounting controls, or auditing matters" and set up a process for confidential, anonymous submission by employees "of concerns regarding questionable accounting or auditing matters." (Because of this requirement, many companies assign responsibility for oversight of the business's compliance programs generally to the audit committee. Firms that chose not to do so, typically so as to avoid overloading the audit committee's members with work, commonly assign this task to the nominating and corporate governance committee.)

- The audit committee must have the power to engage independent counsel and other advisors and to pay such advisors.

- The committee must have the power to set the compensation of the outside auditor.

- At least once a year, the committee must receive a report from the outside auditor on the adequacy of the company's internal controls.

- The committee is to review the company's annual and quarterly disclosure reports, specifically including the MD&A section, as well as the financial statements.

- The committee is to review earnings announcements and other guidance provided analysts.
- The committee must meet periodically in executive session with both the company's internal and outside auditors.
- The committee must review any disagreements between management and the auditors.

The NASDAQ rules are less detailed but substantially similar to the NYSE provisions. (You can review the NASDAQ rules at *http://nasd.complinet.com/nasd/display/display.html?rbid =1189&element_id=1159000635.*)

SAMPLE AUDIT COMMITTEE CHARTERS

Several good sample audit committee charters are available online:

The IIA research Foundation: *www.theiia.org/iia/aboutthe iia/research/SampleACCharterSarboxfinal.pdf*

AICPA: *www.aicpa.org/audcommctr/toolkitsnpo/Consolidated _Matrix.htm*

Key Guidelines

Accounting firm KPMG offers the following "basic principles" that should guide the audit committee's members:

1. Recognize that the dynamics of each company, board, and audit committee are unique—one size does not fit all.
2. The board must ensure the audit committee comprises the "right" individuals to provide independent oversight.

3. The board and audit committee must continually assert that, and assess whether, the "tone at the top" embodies insistence on integrity and accuracy in financial reporting.

4. The audit committee must demand and continually reinforce the "direct responsibility" of the external auditor to the board and audit committee as representatives of the shareholders (as is now required by the Sarbanes-Oxley Act).

5. Audit committees must implement a process that supports their understanding and monitoring of the:
   - specific role of the audit committee in relation to the specific roles of the other participants in the financial reporting process (oversight);
   - critical financial reporting risks;
   - effectiveness of financial reporting controls;
   - independence, accountability, and effectiveness of the external auditor; and
   - transparency of financial reporting.

Other Audit Committee Duties

The audit committee is SOX's central clearinghouse. As we've reviewed SOX's various provisions, we've seen numerous duties imposed on the audit committee. The audit committee must approve any nonaudit services performed by the company's outside certified public accounting firm. The audit committee supervises the company's whistle-blower policies. The audit committee is required to ensure that the outside auditor can perform its audit unimpeded by management. The audit committee acts as a liaison between management and the outside auditor, especially with respect to any disagreements between them or any other problems that arise during the audit. The audit committee should review the CEO and CFO's certifications with the outside auditor. The audit committee must ensure that every five years the outside auditor rotates both the partner principally responsible for conducting the audit and the partner responsible for reviewing the audit.

SEC Audit Committee Disclosure Rules

The SEC put additional teeth into the exchange's audit committee requirements by mandating that corporate proxy statements include a report from that committee containing a variety of disclosures. The report, for example, must state whether the committee reviewed and discussed the company's audited financial statements with management and the firm's independent auditors. The report also must state whether the audit committee recommended to the board of directors that the audited financial statements be included in the company's annual report on Form 10-K.

The Oversight Duties of the Board

In addition to the specific mandates of SOX and the stock exchange listing requirements, directors also must comply with their state corporation law fiduciary duties. Generally, corporate directors and officers owe their firm and its shareholders three basic fiduciary duties: care, loyalty, and good faith. Of these, the duty of care is most relevant for present purposes. According to the Delaware courts, the duty of care requires corporate directors to exercise "that amount of care which ordinarily careful and prudent men would use in similar circumstances." Central to the duty of care is an obligation for directors and officers to avail themselves, prior to making a business decision, of all material information reasonably available to them.

Watching for Red Flags

A Delaware court opinion on the responsibilities of audit committees held that there is no liability possible unless "the audit committee had clear notice of serious accounting irregularities and simply chose to ignore them or, even worse, to encourage their continuation." This suggests that the audit committee's main task is to keep an eye open for red flags.

KPMG accounting partner Kenneth Daly suggests the following common red flags an audit committee needs to give particular attention to:

- Complex business arrangements not well understood and appearing to serve little practical purpose
- Financial results that seem "too good to be true" or significantly better than those of competitors—without substantive differences in operations
- Apparent inconsistencies between the facts underlying the financial statements, president's letter, and MD&A
- A consistently close or exact match between reported results and planned results—for example, results that always are exactly on budget or managers who always achieve 100 percent of bonus opportunities
- A pattern of shipping most of the month's or quarter's sales in the last week or on the last day
- Unusual balance sheet changes or changes in trends or important financial statement relationships—for example, receivables growing faster than revenue or accounts payable that are consistently delayed
- Unusual accounting policies, particularly for revenue recognition and cost deferrals—for example, recognizing revenue before products have been shipped or deferring items that normally are expensed as incurred

- Accounting principles or practices at variance with industry norms
- Use of reserves to smooth out earnings—for example, large additions to reserves that are reversed in a later period
- Frequent and significant changes in estimates for no apparent reasons, increasing or decreasing reported earnings

Setting an Appropriate Tone at the Top

As a matter of good corporate practice, an audit committee therefore should establish a "tone at the top" that encourages honesty, integrity, and compliance with legal requirements. In particular, members of an audit committee should not passively rely on management and the outside auditors. While members of the audit committee are not private investigators charged with conducting corporate espionage to detect wrongdoing, they are obliged to make a candid inquiry before accepting the reports they receive from management and outside auditors. As the Delaware Supreme Court observed in *Smith v. Van Gorkom*, the board must "proceed with a critical eye in assessing information" provided by others.

7

Accounting, Internal Controls, and Audits

Enron was primarily an accounting scandal, little different from the 150-plus other accounting fraud cases that the SEC investigates in most years. Indeed, this was true not just of Enron, but also most of the other recent corporate scandals. Management relied upon the substantial flexibility inherent in GAAP to manage earnings and manipulate financial data so that operating results conformed to forecasts. The goal was to keep the firm's stock price high so that the managers could profit from their stock options. Because a standard accounting audit is not a true forensic audit designed to uncover wrongdoing, but rather only a sampling audit that may entirely miss the problem, and because at least some accountants chose to overlook problems, many managers thought they could get away with cooking the books.

Not surprisingly, much of Sarbanes-Oxley is concerned with auditing and accounting. Congress set out to reform the accounting industry by establishing the PCAOB as a new regulator with real teeth. Congress also sought to remake the relationship between auditor and corporate client so as to reduce the conflicts of interest inherent in that relationship. Finally, Congress sought to reshape the intrafirm accounting process, by imposing new rules on the audit committee (see the previous chapter) and the firm's internal control systems.

The PCAOB

Prior to Sarbanes-Oxley, the accounting profession was largely self-regulating. The key actors—FASB and the AICPA—were private sector entities subject to minimal SEC oversight. FASB set accounting standards, while the AICPA provided guidance and contributed to the development of generally accepted principles and standards.

SOX shook up that cozy little world in a big way. Section 101 established the PCAOB as a nonprofit corporation to "oversee the audit of public companies that are subject to the securities laws." Funding for its operations comes from a special tax—called an accounting support fee—on public corporations. The fee varies with company size, specifically with the company's "average monthly U.S. equity market capitalization," so that larger firms bear a higher share of the burden.

The five members of the PCAOB's board must be "prominent individuals of integrity and reputation who have a demonstrated commitment to the interests of investors and the public," no more than two of whom can be CPAs. The SEC appoints the board members, in consultation with the chairman of the Federal Reserve Board and the secretary of the Treasury. The members serve five-year terms. The SEC can remove board members for good cause. The chairman of the board may not have been a practicing CPA within the five years prior to his or her appointment. While serving as a PCAOB board member, no one may receive payments from a public accounting firm other than fixed retirement income.

SOX § 101(c) specifies the PCAOB's duties, the most important of which are:

1. Develop a system for registration of public accounting firms that prepare audit reports for reporting companies. Per SOX § 102, only registered accounting firms can audit the books of reporting companies. In order to register, an accounting firm must make extensive disclosures about its clients, fees, and practices, as well as consent to cooperate in any PCAOB investigation.

2. Establish standards governing auditing, quality control, ethics, independence, and other matters relating to the preparation of audit reports for reporting companies.

3. Conduct regular inspections of registered public accounting firms to ensure that the firms are complying with PCAOB and SEC rules. Large accounting firms (with more than 100 reporting company clients) get inspected annually, while smaller ones are inspected every three years. If the PCAOB finds any violations, it reports them to the SEC and any relevant state accountant licensing board. Even if the PCAOB finds no violations, it still must send a written report to the SEC and the relevant state agencies.

4. Conduct investigations and disciplinary proceedings of misconduct by registered public accounting firms and any individuals associated with such firms. The PCAOB can impose a wide range of sanctions on violators, up to and including permanent revocation of the right to conduct audits of reporting companies.

For more information about the PCAOB, visit their Web site: *www.pcaob.org/About_the_PCAOB/index.aspx.*

The Relationship Between the PCAOB and FASB

Sarbanes-Oxley § 103 gives the PCAOB what the Senate committee report on the act called "plenary authority" to set accounting standards. The PCAOB thus can adopt, amend, or pre-empt guidance issued by the AICPA and other private sector groups. To date, except where SOX clearly requires otherwise, the PCAOB mostly has simply adopted the pre-existing standards set by the AICPA. In effect, however, the act downgrades the AICPA's role in the standard-setting process to merely advisory.

A mid-2004 change in how audit reports are drafted forcefully illustrated the PCAOB's new predominance in the standard-setting area. In the past, a reporting company's auditors would certify that the audit was conducted in accordance with GAAS and that the financial statements fairly and accurately represented the company's condition in accordance with GAAP. Since May 2004, however, the PCAOB requires audit reports to state that the audit and financial statements comply with "the standards of the Public Company Accounting Oversight Board."

The PCAOB doesn't have the field entirely to itself, however. SOX § 108 authorizes the SEC to "recognize, as 'generally accepted' for purposes of the securities laws, any accounting principles established by a standard setting body" that meets the following conditions:

- The body is a private entity.
- The body is governed by a board of trustees, the majority of whom are not, or have not been during the past two years, associated with any registered public accounting firm.
- The body "has adopted procedures to ensure prompt consideration, by majority vote of its members, of changes to accounting principles necessary to reflect emerging accounting issues and changing business practices" and "considers, in adopting accounting principles, the need to keep standards current in order to reflect changes in the business environment, the extent to which international

convergence on high quality accounting standards is necessary or appropriate in the public interest and for the protection of investors."

- The SEC determines that the body has the capacity to assist the commission in carrying out its duties "because, at a minimum, the standard setting body is capable of improving the accuracy and effectiveness of financial reporting and the protection of investors under the securities laws."

In April 2003, the SEC recognized FASB as such a standard-setting body. Accordingly, FASB now receives funding from the same user fees that support the PCAOB. In addition, FASB functions as a separate standard setter working in parallel with the PCAOB.

The relationships between the SEC, PCAOB, FASB, and AICPA are fraught with the potential for conflict. To date, the three private sector entities have managed to work together in a reasonably cooperative manner. In general, the PCAOB has primary responsibility for GAAS, the FASB for GAAP, and the AICPA for nonreporting company accounting rules, but there seems to be a good deal of mutual consultation. In the event of conflict, of course, the SEC's oversight role gives it the last word.

The PCAOB and State Licensing

Like lawyers, physicians, dentists, and various other professionals, accountants traditionally are licensed for practice by states rather than the federal government. The PCAOB does not displace this system of state licensing and regulation. Instead, the two work in tandem. A CPA thus must be licensed by the state to practice accounting; if the CPA's practice includes auditing the books of reporting companies, the CPA's accounting firm also must be registered with the PCAOB.

PCAOB standards governing auditing of reporting companies will pre-empt any contrary state regulations, but this leaves the states as the primary regulator for audits of nonreporting companies. In general, of course, states simply mandate compliance with GAAS and GAAP.

There's clearly a need for effective coordination between the PCAOB and state licensing bodies, both so that accounting practices and auditing standards remain reasonably uniform across all types of companies and so that individuals or firms disciplined at one level are also investigated at the other. Here, again, is a role for the SEC to use its oversight authority to encourage such cooperation.

New Rules for the Auditor-Client Relationship

At Enron and other firms, the audit process broke down in part because accountants got too cozy with their clients. Sarbanes-Oxley included a number of provisions designed to put some space back between client and outside auditor.

Limits on Nonaudit Services

As we saw in Chapter 1's review of the business failures of 2000–2002, a key concern motivating SOX's drafters was the conflict of interest inherent when accounting firms sell other services to the corporations whose books they audit. Title II of the act therefore limited the extent to which accountants may provide consulting services to their audit clients. Some nonaudit services were banned outright. The outside auditor, for example, may not provide bookkeeping or related services, design or implement financial information systems, provide fairness opinions in connection with corporate transactions, conduct internal audits on an outsourced basis, provide humans relations services, or act as an investment banker or legal expert. In addition, the PCAOB is authorized to ban other nonaudit services as it deems fit.

DID PROVIDING NONAUDIT SERVICES REALLY COMPROMISE AUDITOR INDEPENDENCE?

Yale law professor Roberta Romano compiled the results of numerous studies of auditor performance and concluded that the "overwhelming majority" "suggest that SOX's prohibition of the purchase of non-audit services from an auditor is an exercise in legislating away a non-problem." Most of the studies found that there was no connection between provision of nonaudit services and the quality of the audit. Several even found that auditors who provided nonaudit services performed higher quality audits, presumably because providing such services gives the auditor more and better information about the company. You can read her analysis at *http://papers.ssrn.com/sol3/papers.cfm?abstract_id=596101.*

Contrary to conventional wisdom, however, SOX did not completely ban all such services. Provided the client's audit committee approves the retention in advance, in fact, the auditor may perform any nonaudit services not banned by SOX or the PCAOB. For example, a corporation's outside auditor can also prepare its corporate tax returns. It's advisable, however, to check with legal counsel before asking the auditor to perform any nonaudit services.

The SEC requires disclosure of any "fees paid to the independent accountant for (1) audit services, (2) audit-related services, (3) tax services, and (4) other services" in the annual report on Form 10-K. The SEC has also cautioned companies that there are "some circumstances where providing certain tax services to an audit client would impair the independence of an accountant, such as representing an audit client in tax court or other situations involving public advocacy."

The SEC did create an exception for *de minimis* nonaudit services, pursuant to which a registered accounting firm still is independent even if it provides nonapproved, nonaudit services. The aggregate compensation for all such services may constitute no more than 5 percent of the total fees paid the auditor by the client during the relevant fiscal year. Once the company recognizes that it is compensating its auditor for nonaudit services without prior approval by the audit committee, the management promptly must bring the oversight to the audit committee's attention and have the services approved by the committee.

Auditors Work for the Audit Committee

As we saw in Chapter 6, SOX significantly expanded the role of the audit committee of the board of directors. Many of these new rules directly affect the reporting company's outside auditor. It is now the audit committee, for example, that must select the reporting company's outside auditor and negotiate the auditor's fees. The audit committee must approve (typically in advance) any nonbanned, nonaudit services the auditor provides to the corporation.

SOX clarified that the outside auditor is responsible to the audit committee, rather than management. The outside auditors must periodically meet with the audit committee outside the presence of management. At least annually, the outside auditor of a NYSE-listed company must give the audit committee a report detailing: (1) the firm's internal control procedures; (2) any material problems identified in the most recent internal control review, or by any government or other regulatory body investigation; (3) any steps taken to deal with any such problems; and (4) all relationships between the independent auditor and the listed company. Obtaining such a report has become best practice for non-NYSE firms, as well.

The auditor should report to the audit committee any disagreement between management and the auditor as to financial reporting. If the disagreement is resolved, the auditor still must report it to the audit committee, and also report on the manner in which it was dealt with. If a dispute is not resolved between management and the auditor, it is up to the audit committee to solve the problem.

Where GAAP provides options as to how to disclose information, the auditor should flag the issue for the audit committee. The auditor should discuss the alternatives with the audit committee and identify the disclosure it preferred.

No Coercing the Auditor

SOX § 303 makes it unlawful for an officer or director of a reporting company, or anyone acting under their orders, to "fraudulently influence, coerce, manipulate, or mislead any independent" CPA "engaged in the performance of an audit" of the company's financial statements "for the purpose of rendering such financial statements materially misleading." The SEC defines *officer* for this purpose as including "the company's 'president, vice president, secretary, treasurer or principal financial officer, comptroller or principal accounting officer, and any person routinely performing corresponding functions.'"

Per the SEC rules implementing § 303, the prohibition doesn't apply just to employees of the reporting company acting under orders from directors or officers of the company:

In other words, someone may be "acting under the direction" of an officer or director even if they are not under the supervision or control of that officer or director. Such persons might include not only the issuer's employees but also, for example, customers, vendors or creditors who, under the direction of an officer or director, provide false or misleading confirmations or other false or misleading information to auditors, or who enter into "side agreements" that enable the issuer to mislead the auditor. In appropriate circumstances, persons acting under the direction of officers and directors also may include not only lower level employees of the issuer but also other partners or employees of the accounting firm (such as consultants or forensic accounting specialists retained by counsel for the issuer) and attorneys, securities professionals, or other advisors who, for example, pressure an auditor to limit the scope of the audit, to issue an unqualified report on the financial statements when such a report would be unwarranted, to not object to an inappropriate accounting treatment, or not to withdraw an issued audit report on the issuer's financial statements.

The SEC likewise has provided guidance as to the kinds of conduct deemed improper influence:

- Offering or paying bribes or other financial incentives, including offering future employment or contracts for nonaudit services
- Providing an auditor with an inaccurate or misleading legal analysis
- Threatening to cancel or canceling existing nonaudit or audit engagements if the auditor objects to the issuer's accounting

- Seeking to have a partner removed from the audit engagement because the partner objects to the issuer's accounting
- Blackmailing or making physical threats

This list is not exclusive and under appropriate circumstances other conduct could be a violation. Among other potentially prohibited conduct is "knowingly providing to the auditor inadequate or misleading information that is key to the audit, transferring managers or principals from the audit engagement, and when predicated by an intent to defraud, verbal abuse, creating undue time pressure on the auditors, not providing information to auditors on a timely basis, and not being available to discuss matters with auditors on a timely basis."

Miscellaneous Rules

Congress considered requiring reporting companies to rotate their outside auditor periodically, but ultimately decided not to go that route. Instead, SOX § 203 requires registered public accounting firms to rotate (1) the partner having primary responsibility for the audit and (2) the partner responsible for reviewing the audit every five years. The audit committee must ensure that the requisite rotation actually takes place.

As a matter of good practice, a company ought to consider rotating audit firms periodically so as to get the benefit of a fresh set of eyes. Some corporate governance experts recommend doing so at least every ten years. In addition, governance experts recommend rotating audit firms if a substantial number of former company employees have gone to work for the audit firm or vice-versa.

A separate rule imposes a cooling-off period, pursuant to which an employee of a registered accounting firm may not go to work for a client on whose audit team the employee served until one year after ceasing to be a member of the audit team.

The registered accounting firm may not compensate an audit partner based on the amount of nonaudit services the client purchases.

The auditor and its employees may not have any financial interest in the client or any business relationship with the client excepting, of course, the audit relationship and any authorized nonaudit services.

Finally, SOX requires that registered accounting firms retain records relating to audits of reporting companies for at least seven years. The prohibition applies to both shredding of physical documents and purging of electronic records. It also applies to all work papers and other interim documentation, as well as final reports.

General Standards of Auditor Independence

In addition to the specific rules we've been reviewing in this section, the SEC set up a backstop—a general expectation of auditor independence. According to the SEC, an auditor's independence is impaired either when the accountant is not in fact independent or when a reasonable investor would conclude, in light of the relevant facts and circumstances, that the auditor would not be capable of acting independently. Hence, any mutual or conflicting interest with the audit client would impair the auditor's independence. In addition, an independent auditor must recognize its obligations not only to management and the shareholders, but also to creditors and other corporate constituencies that rely on the objectivity of the company's financial statements.

Section 404: Internal Controls

For the board of directors and top management of a public corporation to discharge their obligations to oversee the financial reporting process, they must identify, understand, and assess the factors that may cause the financial statements to be fraudulently misstated. Sarbanes-Oxley § 404 creates an obligation to do so having real teeth:

§ 404. Management Assessment of Internal Controls

(a) Rules Required.—The Commission shall prescribe rules requiring each annual report . . . to contain an internal control report, which shall—

(1) state the responsibility of management for establishing and maintaining an adequate internal control structure and procedures for financial reporting; and

(2) contain an assessment, as of the end of the most recent fiscal year of the issuer, of the effectiveness of the internal control structure and procedures of the issuer for financial reporting.

(b) Internal Control Evaluation and Reporting.—With respect to the internal control assessment required by subsection (a), each registered public accounting firm that prepares or issues the audit report for the issuer shall attest to, and report on, the assessment made by the management of the issuer. An attestation made under this subsection shall be made in accordance with standards for attestation engagements issued or adopted by the Board. Any such attestation shall not be the subject of a separate engagement.

If you parse that text, § 404 looks at first like a mere disclosure requirement. It requires inclusion of internal control disclosures in each public corporation's annual report. This disclosure statement must include: (1) a written confirmation by which firm management acknowledges its responsibility for establishing and maintaining a system of internal controls and procedures for financial reporting; (2) an assessment, as of the end of the most recent fiscal year, of the effectiveness of the firm's internal controls; and (3) a written attestation by the firm's outside auditor confirming the adequacy and accuracy of those controls and procedures. It's not the disclosure itself that makes § 404 a headache, of course; instead, the problem is the need to assess and test the company's internal controls in order to be able to make the required disclosures.

Make no mistake; § 404 really is a headache. Study after study confirms that Section 404 has imposed huge costs on American business. According to a 2003 article in *USA Today*, for example, the CEOs of Affiliated Computer Services and Steelcase both said that their companies will spend 20,000 staff hours to comply with § 404, which is the equivalent of ten people working full-time for a year! (When SOX was under consideration, the SEC estimated only 383 staff hours would be required, which has proven to be one of the more laughable underestimates in recent memory.) A survey by Foley & Lardner found that the average cost of being public for a company with annual revenue under $1 billion increased by $1.6 million—130 percent—after SOX went into force. And because a lot of SOX § 404 compliance costs are fixed—that is, they don't depend on firm size—the cost of complying weighs especially heavily on smaller firms (see Chapter 1, page 5).

Internal Controls Defined

During the Congressional hearings that led up to Sarbanes-Oxley, internal controls generated most of the buzz. Enron, WorldCom, and most of the world's other ills were blamed on failed internal controls. Not surprisingly, they got a lot of attention from Congress.

Unfortunately, the phrase *internal controls* has a long and contested meaning in the accounting profession. Worse yet, Congress compounded the problem by using the phrase in two different sections of SOX with very different meanings.

As we saw in Chapter 3, SOX § 302 requires a reporting company's CEO and CFO to certify, among other things, that the company has "internal controls to ensure that material information relating to the issuer and its consolidated subsidiaries is made known to such officers by others within those entities." In a June 2003 statement, the SEC explained that internal controls as used in § 302 therefore refers to "disclosure controls and procedures," which the SEC in turn defined "to mean controls and procedures of a company that are designed to ensure that information required to be disclosed by the company in the reports that it files or submits under the Exchange Act is recorded, processed, summarized and reported, within the time periods specified in the Commission's rules and forms." In other words, for purposes of a § 302 certification, the question is whether the company has established appropriate procedures to ensure that the information contained in documents like the 10-K and 10-Q reports is accurate and complete.

In contrast, § 404 refers to "internal control structure and procedures for financial reporting." According to the SEC, the set of internal controls to which § 404 refers is narrower than those dealt with under § 302. Specifically, the SEC defines "internal control" for purposes of § 404 as:

A process designed by, or under the supervision of, the registrant's principal executive and principal financial officers, or persons performing similar functions, and effected by the registrant's board of directors, management and other personnel, to provide reasonable assurance regarding the reliability of financial reporting and the preparation of financial statements for external purposes in accordance with generally accepted accounting principles and includes those policies and procedures that

- pertain to the maintenance of records that in reasonable detail accurately and fairly reflect the transactions and dispositions of the assets of the registrant;
- provide reasonable assurance that transactions are recorded as necessary to permit preparation of financial statements in accordance with generally accepted accounting principles, and receipts and expenditures of the registrant are being made only in accordance with authorizations of management and directors of the registrant; and
- provide reasonable assurance regarding prevention or timely detection of unauthorized acquisition, use or disposition of the registrant's assets that could have a material effect on the financial statements.

In other words, the term *internal controls* as used in § 404 refers to the processes the company uses to ensure that its financial statements comply with GAAP and are free from material misrepresentations and omissions.

Basic Principles for Assessing Internal Controls

According to the SEC guidance proposed in December 2006, management's assessment per § 404 is to be guided by two basic principles. First, management should evaluate the company's existing internal controls over financial reporting to determine whether there is a reasonable possibility that those controls would not prevent or detect a material misstatement in the financial statements. Management need not assess all of the various internal controls or other law compliance programs the company may have implemented, but rather should focus on those controls intended or necessary to prevent or detect such a material misstatement. In adopting this principle, the SEC stressed that a considerable portion of the unexpectedly high costs of complying with § 404 are attributable to excessive testing of controls.

Second, management's assessment of the design and operation of the company's internal controls over financial reporting should be risk based. Put another way, management focuses its evaluation on those areas of financial reporting that pose the greatest risks of material errors in the company's financial disclosures.

To assist companies in implementing these principles, the SEC identifies four basic components of the § 404 compliance process. First, management should identify the principal risks to accurate financial disclosures posed by its business and the existing controls, if any, designed to address those risks. As such, the SEC's guidance reflects the principle of a risk-based approach to internal controls. Implementing that principle requires management to exercise judgment in separating those areas of its accounting and financial reporting operations that are both material and by their nature present a risk of intentional or negligent errors in financial reporting. The SEC explains that "financial reporting elements would generally have higher risk when they include transactions, account balances or other supporting information that is prone to misstatement. For example, elements which: (1) involve judgment in determining the recorded amounts; (2) are susceptible to fraud; (3) have complexity in the underlying accounting requirements; or (4) are subject to environmental factors, such as technological and/or economic developments, would generally be assessed as higher risk." The SEC calls particular attention to those areas "involving significant accounting estimates, related party transactions, or critical accounting policies," which generally should be assessed as having "higher risk for both the risk of material misstatement to the financial reporting element and the risk of control failure." Having identified the areas of high risk, management then must identify the existing controls designed to reduce the risk of a material misstatement in these areas. Only those controls must be included in management's § 404 assessment report.

Second, once management has identified the controls that must be assessed, management then gathers and analyzes evidence as to whether those controls are effective in preventing or timely detecting financial reporting fraud or errors. Although management's § 404 assessment report is based on whether any material weaknesses exist as of the end of the fiscal year, the SEC's guidance encourages management to exercise informed judgment in adapting its existing daily business, self-assessment, and other monitoring activities to provide the basis for its § 404 assessment report. According to the SEC, tying the § 404 assessment to existing compliance activities will reduce costs by obviating the need for an annual internal § 404 audit.

Third, based on the evidence it gathers in the second phase, management must determine whether there are any deficiencies in its internal controls. If so, management must decide whether the identified deficiencies are material weaknesses. For this purpose, the SEC defines a material weakness as "a deficiency, or combination of deficiencies, in ICFR such that there is a reasonable possibility that a material misstatement of the company's annual or interim financial statements will not be prevented or detected on a timely basis by the company's ICFR." If a deficiency rises to the level of a material weakness, management's assessment report must state that the company's internal controls over financial reporting are not effective.

Finally, management must document the processes by which its assessment report was prepared and the evidence it gathered and evaluated in the course of its assessment. The SEC encourages management to exercise informed judgment in deciding the form the documentation will take. In practice, as discussed below, most companies rely on the emerging suites of § 404 compliance software tools to provide the requisite documentation.

Selecting a Framework for Conducting the § 404 Assessment

The SEC rules implementing § 404 require that all reporting company managers base their assessment on "a suitable, recognized control framework." The only framework for conducting the assessment to date approved by the SEC is the Internal Control–Integrated Framework (ICIF), which was promulgated by the Committee of Sponsoring Organizations of the Treadway Commission (COSO). Unfortunately, while the COSO framework sets out the elements of an effective internal control system, it provides very limited directions on how actually to go about evaluating the company's internal controls over financial reporting.

The COSO framework sets out three broad areas in which companies should have systems of internal control: the reliability of the company's financial reporting, the effectiveness and efficiency of company operations, and the company's compliance with applicable laws and regulations. Section 404 and the SEC rules thereunder, of course, only mandate corporate compliance with the first area.

The COSO framework evaluates company performance with respect to each of the base objectives using five components: risk assessment, control environment, control activities, information and communication, and monitoring. COSO further broke down these components to set out twenty basic principles:

Control Environment

1. Integrity and Ethical Values. Sound integrity and ethical values, particularly of top management, are developed and understood and set the standard of conduct for financial reporting.
2. Board of Directors. The board of directors understands and exercises oversight responsibility related to financial reporting and related internal control.
3. Management's Philosophy and Operating Style. Management's philosophy and operating style support achieving effective ICFR [i.e., internal controls for financial reporting].
4. Organizational Structure. The company's organizational structure supports effective ICFR.
5. Financial Reporting Competencies. The company retains individuals competent in financial reporting and related oversight roles.
6. Authority and Responsibility. Management and employees are assigned appropriate levels of authority and responsibility to facilitate effective ICFR.
7. Human Resources. Human resource policies and practices are designed and implemented to facilitate effective ICFR.

Risk Assessment

8. Financial Reporting Objectives. Management specifies financial reporting objectives with sufficient clarity and criteria to enable the identification of risks to reliable financial reporting.
9. Financial Reporting Risks. The company identifies and analyzes risks to the achievement of financial reporting

objectives as a basis for determining how the risks should be managed.

10. Fraud Risk. The potential for material misstatement due to fraud is explicitly considered in assessing risks to the achievement of financial reporting objectives.

Activities

11. Integration with Risk Assessment. Actions are taken to address risks to the achievement of financial reporting objectives.

12. Selection and Development of Control Activities. Control activities are selected and developed considering their cost and their potential effectiveness in mitigating risks to the achievement of financial reporting objectives.

13. Policies and Procedures. Policies related to reliable financial reporting are established and communicated throughout the company, with corresponding procedures resulting in management directives being carried out.

14. Information Technology. Information technology controls, where applicable, are designed and implemented to support the achievement of financial reporting objectives.

Information and Communication

15. Financial Reporting Information. Pertinent information is identified, captured, used at all levels of the company, and distributed in a form and timeframe that supports the achievement of financial reporting objectives.

16. Internal Control Information. Information used to execute other control components is identified, captured, and distributed in a form and timeframe that

enables personnel to carry out their internal control responsibilities.

17. Internal Communication. Communications enable and support understanding and execution of internal control objectives, processes, and individual responsibilities at all levels of the organization.

18. External Communication. Matters affecting the achievement of financial reporting objectives are communicated with outside parties.

Monitoring

19. Ongoing and Separate Evaluations. Ongoing and/or separate evaluations enable management to determine whether ICFR is present and functioning.

20. Reporting Deficiencies. Internal control deficiencies are identified and communicated in a timely manner to those parties responsible for taking corrective action, and to management and the board as appropriate.

In order to operationalize the generalities of the COSO framework, most reporting companies have looked to PCAOB Auditing Standard No. 2, which sets out the standards by which PCAOB-registered auditors are to conduct "An Audit of Internal Control Over Financial Reporting Performed in Conjunction with an Audit of Financial Statements." Although Audit Standard No. 2 is intended for use by, and solely binding on, auditors, according to the SEC "many companies indicated that the scope of their management's evaluation process and the methods and procedures used for testing controls were modeled after its requirements."

PCAOB Auditing Standard No. 2 is available at *www.pcaobus.org/Standards/Standards_and_Related_Rules/Auditing_*

Standard_No.2.aspx. The PCAOB also makes an extensive set of questions and answers about Auditing Standard No. 2 available online at *www.pcaob.org/Standards/Staff_Questions_and_Answers/index.aspx.*

In addition to providing a framework for conducting the assessment mandated by § 404, PCAOB Auditing Standard No. 2 also imposes four specific responsibilities on company management:

a. Accept responsibility for the effectiveness of the company's internal control over financial reporting;
b. Evaluate the effectiveness of the company's internal control over financial reporting using suitable control criteria;
c. Support its evaluation with sufficient evidence, including documentation; and
d. Present a written assessment of the effectiveness of the company's internal control over financial reporting as of the end of the company's most recent fiscal year.

COSO AND AS 2 ONLINE

An executive summary of COSO's statement "Internal Control over Financial Reporting—Guidance for Small Public Companies" is available at *www.coso.org/Publications/SB_Executive_Summary.pdf.*

Failure by management to satisfy those obligations will result in adverse opinion by the auditor.

As this book goes to press, the PCAOB is developing a new auditing standard that would:

Direct the auditor to the most important controls and emphasize the importance of risk assessment;

- Revise the definitions of significant deficiency and material weakness, as well as the "strong indicators" of a material weakness;
- Clarify the role of materiality, including interim materiality, in the audit;
- Remove the requirement to evaluate management's process;
- Permit consideration of knowledge obtained during previous audits;
- Direct the auditor to tailor the audit to reflect the attributes of smaller and less complex companies;
- Refocus the multi-location testing requirements on risk rather than coverage; and
- Recalibrate the walkthrough requirement.

As with the SEC guidance issued at roughly the same time, the goal is to reduce compliance costs by focusing Section 404 audits on those areas most likely to result in material misstatements or omissions in the company's financial statements. Because auditors still must annually opine on the effectiveness of their client's internal controls, the extent to which the SEC guidance and PCAOB actions will actually reduce costs will depend in large part how auditors interpret the new standard.

The text of the new auditing standard, as proposed, is available at *www.pcaobus.org/Rules/Docket_021/2006-12-19_Release_No._2006-007.pdf.*

An Overview of § 404 Compliance from Management's Perspective

Section 404 imposes duties on both the management and outside auditor of a reporting company. As the PCAOB explains:

The auditor's report on internal control over financial reporting does not relieve management of its responsibility for assuring users of its financial reports about the effectiveness of internal control over financial reporting.

In this section, we'll take a walk through the § 404 process from management's perspective.

THE AUDIT COMMITTEE'S ROLE

Although § 404 refers to management's responsibility, the audit committee should be an active player in § 404 compliance. KPMG partner Kenneth Daly, in an article for *Risk Management* magazine, recommends that "the audit committee must understand where the company is in the process, as well as the critical elements of the plan that will move the company's compliance program forward. The audit committee should monitor management's progress and ask key questions to help evaluate the state of the section 404 compliance process. It is important to ensure that the right questions are directed to the appropriate management personnel. For example, if the audit committee wants to know whether internal audit's resources are adequate, it should ask the director of internal audit, as well as the CFO. Posing the same question to different levels of management and to different managers also may reveal areas of the compliance process that require attention. Questions that audit committees might ask should revolve around process optimization, technology, organization and people, and risk and control."

Whole books have been written on § 404. PCAOB Auditing Standard No. 2 itself weighs in at 220-plus pages, not counting another 150-plus pages of appendixes. In addition, as the SEC stressed, the process necessarily varies from company to company. Accordingly, this section provides a very general overview. Companies preparing to comply with their obligations under § 404 need to consult with legal counsel and their outside auditor before beginning the process.

At the outset, managers responsible for § 404 compliance must recognize that this is a process rather than a project. Although the first year a company must comply with § 404 likely will be the most costly and time consuming, as well as offering the greatest risk of an adverse auditor opinion, both the management assessment and auditor attestation must be performed every year. It's for this reason, of course, that § 404 costs are a recurring item.

One way in which the SEC's 2006 guidance may prove helpful in cost-containment, however, is by reminding management that, while the Section 404 assessment must be undertaken annually, "subsequent evaluations should be more focused on changes in risks and controls rather than identification of all financial reporting risks and the related controls. Further, in each subsequent year, the evidence necessary to reasonably support the assessment will only need to be updated from the prior year(s), not recreated anew." In implementing this guidance, firms should develop processes for creating an institutional memory so that changes in personnel at either the firm or its auditor do not require reinventing the wheel.

Both the PCAOB and SEC emphasize that § 404 requires a top-down approach, a point that was strongly re-emphasized in the 2006 guidance they provided. The § 404 team therefore starts with controls that apply company-wide. The team then evaluates controls that apply to particular business units or functions. Next, the team looks at how particular business units handle significant accounts. Finally, the team evaluates how transactions in those accounts are processed.

PUTTING TOGETHER A § 404 TEAM

HP published a white paper summarizing how it went about complying with § 404. Candidly, the paper is mostly a sales brochure for HP software, but it does have some useful information. For example, we learn that HP set up "a core team consisting of seven professionals who had direct responsibility" for HP's § 404 compliance process. The team leader came from HP's controller's office and included representatives from "Internal Audit, Application Development, Managed Services, and some of the business units." This sort of cross-function, multidisciplinary team is an emerging best practice. Ideally, the team should have some continuity of membership from year-to-year to both hold down costs and develop institutional memory.

Likewise, both the SEC and PCAOB insist that companies should devote most attention to those high-risk areas most likely to result in financial reporting problems, which supposedly allows management to contain costs by focusing on those controls and areas where there is a particular risk of a material misstatement occurring in the company's financial statements. To take a basic example, a COSO study found that over 50 percent of financial fraud involved overstating revenues either by recognizing revenue prematurely or by booking fictitious revenue. A company therefore would be foolish not to devote considerable attention to the internal controls it uses to monitor revenue recognition. Accordingly, we'll use revenue recognition as an example of how the internal control audit might work.

At the company-wide control level, controls for revenue recognition would start with distribution of written policy manuals setting out the rules by which the company recognizes revenue and the procedures for doing so. In addition, the company should mandate regular training of both sales and accounting personnel.

Documentation is an essential part of the internal control assessment. Accordingly, not only copies of the policy manual, but also records of attendance at training sessions should be maintained. There's a growing array of software packages available designed to assist with § 404 compliance, most of which include some sort of database system for maintaining electronic copies of the requisite documentation.

OTHER HIGH RISK AREAS

In addition to revenue recognition, four other areas have proven especially common sources of financial fraud: (1) stock options and other issuance of equity securities, (2) accounting for reserves, accruals, and contingencies, (3) capitalization of expenses, and (4) inventory levels. All of these are areas where attention should be devoted during the § 404 assessment process.

Moving down the ladder from the company-wide to the business-unit level, one next would look at large, one-time, or otherwise unique contracts that account for a material share of the company's revenues. An adequate system of internal control requires that the company's internal auditors review the terms of the contract to determine when and how revenues from it should be recognized. In addition, internal audit should double-check the work of the business unit, by confirming the details of the contract with the other party.

INTERNAL AUDITORS

NYSE-listed companies are required to have an "internal audit function to provide management and the audit committee with ongoing assessments of the company's risk management processes and system of internal control." The company may outsource this function, although not to the company's outside auditor. Among non-NYSE companies, having an internal auditor is becoming a recognized best practice.

The Institute of Internal Auditors, a trade association, explains that: "Although they are independent of the activities they audit, internal auditors are integral to the organization and provide ongoing monitoring and assessment of all activities. On the contrary, external auditors are independent of the organization, and provide an annual opinion on the financial statements." In other words, internal auditors work for management (and the audit committee). At many companies, they play a key role in § 404 compliance.

Note that the SEC's rules on the independence of outside auditors forbid the outside auditor from designing or testing a company's internal controls. This is an important reason for companies to have an internal audit unit.

The next step down will involve looking at how the company handles routine transactions. Suppose you're on the § 404 compliance team at Acme, a manufacturing company. Like most companies, Acme provides quarterly revenue forecasts for stock market analysts. Acme's top management puts a lot of pressure on employees to "make the number." Suppose Acme is basically healthy, but internal projections suggest that it may not meet its earnings forecasts for the first quarter of the year. Quarterly revenue numbers could be tweaked to help the company meet its earnings forecast in a variety of ways. Acme could backdate shipping records, for example, so that revenue for products actually shipped in the second quarter is recognized in the first quarter. Alternatively, products returned in the first quarter might not be booked until the second quarter, so as to delay the resulting hit to earnings. In the worst case, Acme management might actually report fictitious revenue by claiming to have shipped products that never existed.

There are lots of other ways for creative managers under pressure to cook the revenue books. In 2003, for example, the SEC charged that Internet real estate company Homestore artificially inflated revenues through so-called roundtrip deals:

> In these round-trip transactions, Homestore paid inflated sums to various vendors for services or products, and, in turn, the vendors used these funds to buy advertising from two media companies. The media companies then bought advertising from Homestore, and Homestore improperly recorded the money it received from the sale of such advertising as revenue in its financial statements. The essence of these transactions was a circular flow of money by which Homestore recognized its own cash as revenue.

An effective system of internal controls will include procedures for ensuring that the responsible personnel treat these sort of routine transactions properly from an accounting perspective. One important control is a walkthrough, by which the internal auditors (or their equivalent) observe how a sample transaction is processed. In a manufacturing company, there should be mechanisms in place for internal audit to meet with the personnel in charge of shipping and receiving to check on shipments and returns, dating of shipping and return documents, and the like. Similarly, internal audit should check inventory levels.

MORE ON REVENUE RECOGNITION

Revenuerecognition.com offers a wide range of resources dealing with revenue recognition tailored for financial executives.

Internal controls must be effective as to both their design and operation. Accountant Jack Paul, in an online article for *The CPA Journal,* explains the difference between the two as follows:

Whereas design effectiveness pertains to whether a control is properly crafted, operating effectiveness deals with use of a properly designed control to prevent, detect, or correct misstatements or irregularities on a timely basis. For example, a daily reconciliation of cash receipts is not effectively designed when the cashier performs the reconciliation. But if an independent person is designated to perform the reconciliation and the other procedures are properly documented, the control is effectively designed. The control is not operating effectively when the independent reconciler either fails to perform the reconciliation daily or does so in a perfunctory manner. Design effectiveness of this control could be tested by reviewing documentation to ensure that the procedures are satisfactory. Operating effectiveness could be tested by examining the reconciler's initials on the daily reconciliation sheet.

Internal controls can also be divided between those relating to how transactions flow within a company and those that deal with static data, such as account balances. Again, Jack Paul explains:

> Examples of controls relating to transaction flows include approving cash disbursements; prelisting cash receipts; approving credit sales; and matching purchase orders, vendor invoices, and receiving reports when booking accounts payable. Controls over balances (stocks) include periodic reconciliation of bank accounts; reconciliation of subsidiary ledgers with control accounts; procedures for physical inventory counts; and controls governing the periodic preparation of financial statements. Overarching controls include the factors comprising the control environment. Overarching controls and those pertaining to flows operate continuously throughout the fiscal period; controls relating to balances typically operate less frequently. Thus bank accounts are reconciled monthly, whereas controls over cash flows are continuous.

The annual management assessment confirms and documents that these sorts of controls exist and are functioning properly. Increasingly, companies rely on comprehensive software packages both to document and test their internal controls. Many of these packages integrate § 404 compliance with the § 302 certification process, so as to help contain costs.

Using a single software platform/electronic repository to coordinate and document all controls, documentation, test results, and other relevant supporting materials is useful for several reasons. First, it reduces audit fees. You can simply point your outside auditor at a single repository rather than requiring the auditor to check multiple programs across multiple departments. Second, it ensures adequate documentation in case the SEC challenges the company's compliance. Third, it helps ensure that the company retains key financial reporting documents in accordance with SOX's document retention rules. Finally, a common software platform can provide a central enterprise-wide set of controls. The WorldCom scandal nicely illustrates the potential problems that can arise if your company lacks such controls. As described by a federal court:

> A contributing factor that allowed the books to be deliberately falsified without attracting much notice was that the Company's internal controls over the preparation and publication of its financial results were dysfunctional at best, and in some areas controls were missing entirely. WorldCom's accounting systems had not kept pace with the growth in the Company due to its feverish pace of acquisitions and management neglect. Numerous legacy financial systems were being operated by different WorldCom units, and producing consolidated financial statements required patchwork software and significant manual processing. (S.*E.C. v. Worldcom, Inc.,* 2003 WL 22004827 [S.D.N.Y., Aug 26, 2003]).

Indeed, it's partly to prevent such breakdowns that the SEC and PCAOB insist on a top-down approach to § 404 compliance.

1. Lack of an enterprise-wide, executive-driven internal control management program.
2. Lack of a formal enterprise risk management program.

3. Inadequate controls associated with the recording of nonroutine, complex, and unusual transactions.
4. Ineffectively controlled post-merger integration.
5. Lack of effective controls over the IT environment.
6. Ineffective financial reporting and disclosure preparation processes.
7. Lack of formal controls over the financial closing process.
8. Lack of current, consistent, complete, and documented accounting policies and procedures.
9. Inability to evaluate and test controls over outsourced processes.
10. Inadequate board and audit committee understanding of risk and control.

TEN TOP MATERIAL WEAKNESSES

Albert Lilienfeld of Deloitte & Touche LLP, in an article from the collection *Audit Committee Workshop 2005* (a publication of the Practicing Law Institute), offers the above top ten list of potential material weaknesses to which management and auditors should pay particular attention.

Under SEC rules, management cannot claim that its internal controls are effective if one or more material weaknesses exist. In addition, the existence of any material weakness and the steps being taken to correct it must be disclosed in the annual report on Form 10-K. For this purpose, a material weakness is defined by PCAOB Auditing Standard No. 2 as a "significant deficiency, or combination of significant deficiencies, that results in more than a remote likelihood that a material misstatement of the annual or interim financial statements will not be prevented or detected." In turn, significant deficiency is defined as a problem with the company's internal controls that "adversely affects the company's ability to initiate, authorize, record, process, or report external financial data reliably in accordance with generally accepted accounting principles such that there is more than a remote likelihood that a misstatement of the company's annual or interim financial statements that is more than inconsequential will not be prevented or detected." Internal controls do not have to operate perfectly to be considered effective, so long as the problems do not give rise to "more than a remote likelihood" that the company's financial reporting will be materially and adversely affected.

Significant deficiencies do not have to be disclosed, but as a matter of best practice should be addressed. If fixing a significant deficiency requires a material change to either the disclosure procedures certified per § 302 or to the § 404 internal controls over financial reporting, however, those changes must be disclosed. In that event, the significant deficiency motivating the change also should be disclosed.

The Auditor's Opinions

As implemented by PCAOB Auditing Standard No. 2, § 404 requires the reporting company's registered outside auditing firm to issue two opinions: (1) whether management's assessment of the company's internal controls fairly states the condition and effectiveness of those controls and (2) whether the auditor believes that the company has established effective internal controls over financial reporting.

In order for the auditor to issue an unqualified opinion that the company has the requisite effective controls, the auditor must find no material weaknesses in those controls. In contrast, an auditor can issue an unqualified opinion as to management's assessment even if there are material weaknesses, so long as management's assessment disclosed those weaknesses. Recall that the auditor must issue a disclaimer (i.e., decline to express an opinion) if management fails to carry out its responsibilities under § 404 and/or limits the scope of the audit.

DEFINITIONAL CHANGES

As this book went to press, the PCAOB planned three important amendments to the definitions of *significant deficiencies* and *material weaknesses*. First, in both definitions, the term "more than remote likelihood" would be replaced with the term "reasonable possibility." The goal here is to raise the threshold with respect to the likelihood of an occurrence and thus make clear that the mere risk of a misstatement is not enough to violate the standard. Second, in the definition of *material weakness*, the term "a significant deficiency, or combination of significant deficiencies" will be replaced with the term "a control deficiency, or combination of control deficiencies"; the goal is to make clear that auditors are not required "to search for deficiencies that, individually or in combination, are less severe than material weaknesses." Finally, in the definition of *significant deficiency*, the term "more than inconsequential" will be replaced with the term "significant." The goal here is to prevent auditors from spending "excess time identifying, discussing and fixing deficiencies that are not sufficiently important to the company's overall system of internal control."

The SEC and the PCAOB have emphasized that auditors should integrate their audit of the company's internal controls with their audit of the financial statements, so as to hold down the costs of complying with § 404.

In addition, the PCAOB's proposed amendments to Auditing Standard No. 2 would provide additional cost savings by eliminating the requirement that the auditor conduct an evaluation of management's assessment. As a result, if the proposal is adopted, it will eliminate "the separate opinion on management's assessment because it is redundant of the opinion on internal control itself and because the latter opinion more clearly conveys the same information—specifically, whether the company's internal control is effective."

8

Should You Stay or Should You Go?

SOX compliance isn't cheap. Worse yet, complying with the most expensive provisions—Sections 302 and 404—is an annual event.

There has been a steady stream of public corporations going private to avoid Sarbanes-Oxley. Likewise, many private companies decided to stay private so as to stay out from under SOX.

The trouble is that securities regulation is like a lobster trap. It's easy to get caught and hard to get out.

Whether your company ought to go—or stay—private is a difficult decision. You have to weigh the costs and benefits of going public, the availability of private capital, and so on, all of which varies from company to company. Advice from lawyers and financial advisors is essential. Therefore, this chapter doesn't try to tell you whether to go private, but instead, tells you *how* to go—or stay—private if that's what you decide.

Don't Be a Reporting Company

Because SOX applies only to reporting companies, the only way to get out from under SOX is to stop being a reporting company. Conversely, of course, the only way to avoid getting into the SOX lobster trap is to avoid becoming a reporting a company.

THE DISADVANTAGES OF GOING DARK

Although going private gets one out from under Sarbanes-Oxley, the SEC's periodic reporting rules, stock exchange listing requirements, and various other cost sources, it does have some significant disadvantages. One significant disadvantage is that the company's stock and bonds become illiquid. The company loses access to the capital markets as a source of financing. It will find that equity-based compensation plans become less attractive. For example, closely held corporations with an employee stock ownership plan (ESOP) must have their shares appraised annually. Lastly, going private transactions frequently trigger litigation by aggrieved shareholders.

We touched on the definition of reporting company in Chapter 1. Now we need to dive in.

There are three relevant statutory provisions we need to deal with. First, Securities Exchange Act § 12(a):

It shall be unlawful for any member, broker, or dealer to effect any transaction in any security (other than an exempted security) on a national securities exchange unless a registration is effective as to such security for such exchange in accordance with the provisions of this title and the rules and regulations thereunder.

In other words, if a company has any of its securities—whether equity or debt—listed for trading on the NYSE, AMEX, or any of the eight other national securities exchanges, the company must register that class of security with the SEC using Form 10. Once the company has registered one or more classes, it becomes a reporting company.

Second, Securities Act § 12(g) can pick up larger companies even if they aren't listed for trading on a stock exchange. Under it and SEC Rule 12g-3, any company that has a class of equity securities with 500 or more record holders and total assets of more than $10 million is a reporting company. Unlike § 12(a), only equity securities matter here.

A company typically has far fewer shareholders of record than the actual number of stockholders. When investors buy stock of public corporations through a broker, their shares typically are registered in so-called "street name." The broker places those shares in the custody of a depository firm, such as Depository Trust Co., which then uses a so-called "nominee" to register the shares with the issuer. The broker, of course, retains records identifying the beneficial owner of the shares.

THE OTHER EXCHANGES

In addition to the NYSE and AMEX, there are eight other national securities exchanges registered with the SEC: the Boston Stock Exchange, the Chicago Board Options Exchange, the Chicago Stock Exchange, the International Securities Exchange, the National Stock Exchange (formerly the Cincinnati Stock Exchange), the NASDAQ Stock Market, the Pacific Exchange, and the Philadelphia Stock Exchange.

As a result, a public corporation's list of record shareholders will consist mostly of street names—that is, the names of the nominees used by the various depository firms—not the names of the actual beneficial owners. This means that the vast majority of shareholders will not count against the 500 total required for a company to be captured by § 12(g).

REGISTERED COMPANIES VERSUS REGISTERED SECURITIES

You'll hear it said that the Securities Exchange Act registers companies, while the Securities Act registers securities. In fact, the former registers classes of securities, but the saying otherwise holds true. Accordingly, a corporation that has registered a class of securities under the Securities Exchange Act must nevertheless register a particular offering of securities of that class under the Securities Act or find an exemption from registration before starting to sell additional securities of that class.

The third and final group of reporting companies is identified by Securities Exchange Act § 15(d), which picks up any issuer that makes a registered public offering of securities under the Securities Act of 1933. Unlike § 12(g), this provision applies to both debt and equity securities. As a result, a closely held corporation that makes a public offering of bonds or notes becomes a reporting company. If the issuer has less than 300 record holders of the security offered to the public, the issuer becomes a reporting company only during the fiscal year in which it makes an offering.

When you put these provisions together, getting out from under SOX—or staying out from under it—can require one or more of the following:

- If your company has any class of security, whether common stock, preferred stock, bonds, debentures, notes, or otherwise, listed for trading on a national securities exchange, any such class of securities must be delisted. In other words, you have to ask the exchange to stop making a market in that class of securities. Note that this may not be enough, because one of the other two provisions still could pick up your company.
- If your company has made a registered public offering of either debt or equity securities (say, bonds or stock), you must get the number of holders of record of that security down below 300. Going forward, your company can't make any new public offerings of any type of security, because that would make it a reporting company for one year under § 15(d) even if there are fewer than 300 holders of record.
- If your company isn't listed on a national securities exchange and hasn't made a public offering of securities, but has more than $10 million in assets and more than 500 record shareholders, your company needs to eliminate enough of those record shareholders to get below the magic 500 number. Once it does so, it will cease to be a reporting company.

Getting Delisted

A stock exchange can kick one of its listed companies off the market—that is, delist the securities the company trades on the market—for a lot of reasons. In most years, however, the bulk of delistings are voluntary. In turn, there can be many reasons for a company to voluntarily "go dark," as the saying goes, including for reasons such as being acquired in a merger or takeover, moving to another exchange, or going private. Here, only the latter concerns us.

DOES GOING DARK MEAN GOING COMPLETELY PRIVATE?

Companies that want to maintain a market for their securities after going private have one option: the pink sheets. In the old days, this was the very bottom of the over-the-counter market. At the end of every trading day, the closing prices of the listed companies' stock were published on pink sheets of paper available to dealers and market makers. (Bond prices were printed on yellow sheets.) Today, the pink sheet market has moved online at *www.pinksheets.com*.

NYSE Listed Company Manual § 806.02 states that:

An issuer may delist a security from the Exchange after its board approves the action and the issuer (i) furnishes the Exchange with a copy of the Board resolution authorizing such delisting certified by the secretary of the issuer and (ii) complies with all of the requirements of Rule 12d2-2(c) under the Securities Exchange Act of 1934. The issuer must thereafter file a Form 25 with the Securities and Exchange Commission to withdraw the security from listing on the Exchange and from registration under the Securities Exchange Act of 1934. In addition, the company must provide a copy of the Form 25 to the Exchange simultaneously with the filing of such Form 25 with the Securities and Exchange Commission. If an issuer delists a class of stock from the Exchange pursuant to this Section 806.02, but does not delist other classes of listed securities, the Exchange will give consideration to delisting one or more of such other classes.

WHEN CORRPRO WENT DARK

When Corrpro Companies, Inc., delisted from the AMEX, it issued a statement on its Web site at *www.corrpro.com/ press_releases6.htm,* which stated in part:

Joseph P. Lahey, the Company's President and CEO, commented that "the Company's Board of Directors unanimously approved the delisting and deregistration of the Common Shares. The costs and administrative burdens associated with being a reporting company have significantly increased, particularly in light of new SEC and Sarbanes-Oxley requirements. In light of the lack of an active trading market for the Company's stock and the Company's intent not to access the public capital markets for its foreseeable financing needs, the advantages of being a reporting company are outweighed by the significant external and internal costs associated with the reporting requirements for public companies. We believe that delisting and deregistering will significantly reduce expenses, avoid potentially higher future expenses, enable our management to focus more of its time on operating the Company, and create greater value for our shareholders."

The key provision of SEC rule 12d2-2(c) is a publicity requirement: "the issuer must publish notice" of its intention to delist, "along with its reasons for such withdrawal, via a press release and, if it has a publicly accessible Web site, posting such notice on that Web site." The company is delisted ten days after filing the Form 25 and publishing the required notice. The company ceases to be a reporting company effective ninety days after filing the Form 25. In theory, the SEC can prevent a company from delisting where necessary to protect investors, but this is very rare.

The process thus is very straightforward. The company notifies the NYSE of its intent to delist and publishes the required notice via press release and on its Web site. Ten days later, the company files a Form 25 with the SEC. Assuming the SEC doesn't object, which it generally won't unless the company is in trouble with the commission for other reasons, the company is delisted ten days after that and, after an additional eighty days, is no longer a reporting company. The procedure is essentially identical on the other stock exchanges.

Shrinking the Shareholders

As we've seen, delisting is not enough. One must also shrink the number of record security holders, typically via some form of going private transaction. Sometimes management can accomplish this simply by repurchasing stock or debt via open-market purchases or a tender offer, but to ensure accomplishment of the objective it's usually best to structure the deal in ways that give shareholders or bondholders no choice. The two most commonly used techniques are freeze-out mergers and reverse stock splits.

Reverse Stock Splits

In colloquial speech, the term *stock split* is often used to describe a stock dividend in which the number of shares issued equals or exceeds the number of shares outstanding. In legal terms, however, this is a misuse of terminology. A stock dividend is an issuance of authorized but unissued stock to the shareholders and may be effected by the board of directors acting alone. A stock split, in contrast, is effected by amending the articles of incorporation to reduce the par value. Suppose ABC's board wanted to effect a two-to-one split, in which each shareholder will end up owning two "new" shares post-split for every one pre-split share. ABC's board would recommend that the shareholders approve an amendment to the articles of incorporation reducing the par value from $5 to $2.50 per share. Each shareholder will then receive two "new" shares of common stock for each "old" share they previously owned. Because a stock split is effected via a reduction in the par value, it has no impact on the corporation's balance sheet. Accordingly, the board need not redesignate surplus "as capital . . . if shares are being distributed by a corporation pursuant to a split-up or division of its stock rather than as payment of a dividend declared payable in stock of the corporation." This is so because the capital is the aggregate par value of all outstanding shares. Here the number of outstanding shares went up by two but the par value is one-half its former value, so capital is unchanged.

In a reverse stock split, the process is essentially the same except that the company amends its articles to raise the par value or stated value (in the case of no par stock). When Massachusetts company Hycor, Inc., decided to go private via a reverse stock split, for example, it amended the articles to increase the par value from one cent to forty dollars per share.

As with a regular stock split, the transaction had no impact on Hycor's balance sheet. Hycor shareholders, however, received one new post-split share for every 4,000 "old" shares they owned pre-split.

WHO GOES PRIVATE?

The firms deciding to go private tend to be the smallest non-accelerated filers, which makes sense because these are the firms for whom SOX compliance is the highest percentage of revenues. They also tend to have higher than average insider stock ownership. As we'll see, most going-private transactions require shareholder approval, which is easier to get if management and other insiders own a large chunk of voting stock.

What happened, you may ask, to shareholders who owned less than 4,000 shares? If you owned 1,000 shares, would you receive a quarter share? Like most states, Massachusetts allows but does not require a corporation to issue fractional shares. Where a corporate transaction would leave some shareholders with fractional shares, the corporation may cash out the holders of such shares by paying them the fair value of their shares. The effect (and presumably the intent) of Hycor's reverse stock split thus was to squeeze out the firm's minority shareholders, all of whom owned less than 4,000 shares.

Shareholders have some say over reverse stock splits, because amending the articles of incorporation requires a shareholder vote. In addition, shareholders may sue if they believe the cash-out price is too low.

Freeze-Out Mergers

To effect a freeze-out merger, the company's management typically sets up a shell corporation. The shell will have only a few shareholders, usually the top management of the firm. The shell's assets consist of money borrowed from private equity firms and/or investment banks. Management then proposes a merger between the company going private and the shell corporation, using the shell's cash to buy out the target company's shareholders.

A merger combines two corporations to form a single firm. After a merger, only one of the two companies will survive, but that survivor succeeds by operation of law to all of the assets, liabilities, rights, and obligations of the two constituent corporations. In addition, a merger also converts the shares of each constituent corporation into whatever consideration specified in the merger agreement.

Suppose that under the merger agreement the company's shareholders are to receive fifty dollars per share in cash. After the merger takes place, their shares transform by operation of law into a mere IOU for the promised cash payment.

Corporate law originally required unanimous shareholder approval of mergers. The unanimity requirement created serious holdout problems. In the 1800s, most states reduced the necessary vote to a majority of the outstanding shares. A few states have slightly higher vote requirements, such as two-thirds, but none retains the old unanimity requirement.

Taken together, these rules allow the merger to serve as a form of private eminent domain. Assuming the holders of a majority of the shares approved the deal, objecting shareholders cannot stop the deal from taking place.

Although objecting shareholders have no power to block a freeze-out merger, they are not wholly lacking in remedies. When states began moving away from the unanimity requirement, they also created the statutory appraisal proceeding. In brief, appraisal rights give dissenting shareholders the right to have the fair value of their shares determined and paid to them in cash, provided the dissenting shareholder complies with specified procedures. In addition, objecting shareholders often sue, claiming the deal violates management's fiduciary duties. A freeze-out merger must satisfy an "entire fairness" standard, which means management must pay a fair price and deal fairly with the shareholders. Accordingly, legal counsel and independent financial advice are essential in structuring a freeze-out merger.

9

Sarbanes-Oxley and Your Company

Sarbanes-Oxley has fundamentally changed American corporate governance. In the preceding chapters, we've reviewed the major SOX provisions, including:

1. Creation of the PCAOB to oversee auditing
2. Requirement that CEOs and CFOs certify the accuracy of all reports submitted to the SEC
3. Assessment and certification of the company's internal controls
4. Bars on corporate officers and directors from selling stock during "blackout periods"
5. Prohibition against publicly traded companies making loans to their officers and directors
6. New standards on audit committees and director independence
7. Substantially increased fines and penalties (including jail time) for corporate wrongdoing
8. Enhanced protection for whistle blowers
9. New rules on document retention
10. New legal ethics rules for corporate attorneys appearing and practicing before the SEC

These requirements and the host of other Sarbanes-Oxley provisions we've examined are here to stay. There is no real prospect that Congress will revisit SOX any time soon. Regulatory relief from the SEC will be limited to what SEC chairman Chris Cox called, in a September 2006 speech, developing "a framework for assessing internal control over financial reporting for smaller companies . . . that recognizes their characteristics and needs." Until such a framework is in place, the smallest public corporations—that is, the class of reporting companies known as nonaccelerated filers—will continue to be exempted from having to comply with Section 404. In all other respects, however, SOX likely will remain a critical part of the regulatory environment for the foreseeable future.

Accordingly, what should you and your company be doing as SOX turns five? The answer depends, of course, on the type and size of your company. As we've seen, SOX affects four categories of companies:

- Large reporting companies—that is, public companies with a float greater than $75 million who must file periodic reports with the SEC as either accelerated or large accelerated filers.
- Small reporting companies—nonaccelerated filers, which are public companies whose float is less than 75 million.
- Closely held companies whose management is considering taking the company public.
- Larger closely held corporations and nonprofit entities.

Let's look at each category in turn and summarize where they ought to be today in terms of SOX compliance.

Large Public Companies

Publicly held companies whose stock market float exceeds $75 million are now subject to all of SOX's provisions, as well as all of the associated stock exchange listing standards. For employees and directors of these companies, the principal tasks now are keeping current and containing costs.

Keeping current is essential because what constitutes SOX best practices evolves constantly. For example, companies should periodically evaluate the various policies and codes required by SOX to ensure that they are up-to-date with the state of the art in documentation. The polices and processes especially critical in this regard include:

- Document retention and destruction
- Whistle blower protection
- Stock trading blackout period rules
- Financial officer code of ethics
- Preparation of SEC periodic reports and other disclosures, especially ensuring that there is a process in place to monitor for events triggering a requirement of immediate disclosure on Form 8-K

Ongoing training of employees with respect to such policies is equally important. Current employees should receive periodic refreshers on company policy, while new hires should receive both written copies of company policies and training in those relevant to their jobs.

Keeping current also requires ensuring that the company complies with SOX deadlines. As we've seen, for example, companies are required to rotate their lead auditor not less than every five years. With SOX approaching age five, many reporting companies will be facing this deadline in the near future.

Firms also need to keep current by monitoring changes in key SOX-related personnel. Independent members of the board of directors should be interviewed annually to ensure that they continue to satisfy the definition of independence under both SOX and the relevant stock exchange listing standard. This is especially important with respect to members of the audit committee, since we've seen that they are subject to additional requirements over and above those applicable to "ordinary" board members.

Cost containment will continue to focus on the most expensive SOX provisions, especially the certification requirements under § 302 and § 404. Recall that § 302 requires the CEO and CFO to provide a number of certifications with respect to annual or quarterly reports:

1. Individually certify that he or she has reviewed the annual or quarterly report and, to his or her knowledge, the report does not contain any material misrepresentation or omission of material fact.
2. Certify that, to their knowledge, the financial statements and other financial information contained in the report fairly present in all material respects the corporation's financial condition and results of operations for the period covered by the report.
3. Individually acknowledge in writing that they are responsible for establishing and maintaining the corporation's systems of internal controls.
4. Certify that such internal controls ensure that material information properly flows from the corporation's business units to the CEO and CFO.

As we've seen, the now infamous § 404 requires additional certifications to be included in the company's annual report:

1. An acknowledgment that the company's management is responsible for establishing and maintaining the system of internal controls and procedures for financial reporting.
2. An assessment by management, as of the end of the most recent fiscal year, of the effectiveness of the firm's internal controls.
3. An attestation by the firm's outside auditor confirming the adequacy and accuracy of those controls and procedures.

For most large public companies, 2006 was the third year in which they had to provide the § 404 assessments. These companies have experienced some benefits from the internal control certification process, such as elimination of redundant controls that fail to add value and identification of areas in which there were significant control deficiencies. Yet, as we've seen, the costs of complying with § 404 have also been far higher than anyone expected when the statute was written. As we've also seen, because compliance with § 302 and § 404 is an ongoing process, many of the costs imposed by those sections recur annually.

The good news is that many companies are finding ways to contain these costs. Indeed, a spring 2006 survey of reporting companies found that § 404 compliance costs have dropped an average of 30 percent for smaller reporting companies and by almost half for the largest reporting companies.

Much of the process of testing and documenting the requisite internal controls can now be automated via software packages that also generate reports on which the required certifications can be based. At smart companies, the IT department annually checks to ensure that the company's software platform is state of the art.

Companies have also benefited from the SEC and PCAOB's efforts to help contain costs. They have emphasized that the process of testing, documenting, and auditing the company's internal controls can and should focus on areas that pose high risk of fraud or material errors. Looking forward, additional cost savings should be available as the PCAOB revises Auditing Standard No. 2, which governs how auditors prepare their assessment of the company's internal controls. The PCAOB has repeatedly announced that it will be revising Auditing Standard No. 2 so as to help focus the internal control audit on those areas of highest risk and reduce the necessity of assessing and documenting every nook and cranny of the company's finances.

Small Public Companies

Small businesses are the backbone of our economy, as SEC chairman Chris Cox remarked in a September 2006 speech to the Government-Business Forum on Small Business Capital Formation:

> Just how important is small business to America's anything-but-small economy? Well, for starters, there are no fewer than 23.6 million small businesses that represent more than 99.7% of all employers in the United States.
>
> In terms of jobs, small business makes up more than half of the nation's private-sector workforce. Even more astonishing is that small business creates nearly 80% of all new jobs. And as for America's $12 trillion GDP? Not surprisingly, small business creates over half of it.

Cox assured the small businessmen and women in his audience that the SEC is committed to ensuring that "small business has better access to cheaper capital on the most competitive terms possible." Accordingly, he committed to working with small business to ensure that they do not experience the same sort of "high costs" that plagued "the initial application of [SOX §] 404 to larger companies."

The small business community needs to work to hold Chairman Cox's feet to the fire on this commitment. As we've seen, among companies that currently must comply with § 404, compliance costs for smaller firms are disproportionately higher than those of larger ones. At the same time, however, controlling shareholders, managers, and directors of small public corporations need to start preparing for the day when they will be required to be fully SOX-compliant.

At present, of course, nonaccelerated filers are exempted only from § 404's internal controls assessment and certification requirements. All of the other SOX and stock exchange listing standards we've reviewed in the preceding chapters apply in full force to these companies. Accordingly, the advice on keeping current offered large reporting companies in the preceding section applies in full force to smaller reporting companies.

Compliance issues that have been particularly problematic for smaller companies have included:

- Failing to ensure that directors satisfy the independence requirements under SOX and the stock exchange listing standards
- Failing to have the audit committee preapprove proper nonaudit services provided by the company's auditor and/or using the auditor to provide nonaudit services banned by SOX
- Failing to establish adequate complaint procedures for whistle blowers.
- Failing to adjust to the new rules on real-time disclosure both by monitoring for the broader categories of events

requiring such disclosure and complying with the shorter (four-day) period in which such disclosures are to be made

- Making prohibited loans to officers
- Allowing officers to trade during blackout periods

It's critical that smaller reporting companies (and larger ones too, for that matter) develop policies to ensure that employees comply with all SOX provisions and train employees to recognize areas that are especially applicable to their work.

Companies Preparing to Go Public

Sarbanes-Oxley significantly altered the going-public decision by raising the costs of being public. The effect on the U.S. IPO market has been dramatic. Although the U.S. markets traditionally had a huge share of the IPO market (as much as 90 percent), post-SOX there has been a dramatic shift in the IPO market away from the United States. Increasingly, firms going public (especially multinationals) are doing so in London or Frankfurt.

Domestic and international companies considering going public in the United States despite the added costs must begin planning for becoming SOX-compliant very early in the IPO process. At present, a newly public firm has the same SOX compliance obligations as established firms of the same size. In other words, if the newly public company qualifies as either an accelerated or large accelerated filer, the company must comply with all of SOX's provisions. If the company qualifies as a nonaccelerated filer, it is eligible for the exemption for such firms from § 404 compliance, but otherwise must be fully SOX-compliant.

REGULATORY RELIEF TO COME?

The SEC is considering adopting a rule that would exempt newly public corporations of any size from complying with § 404 until the company files its second annual report with the SEC.

As the company plans its IPO, it therefore should take a number of steps to prepare for SOX compliance:

- Consider setting aside cash reserves to meet the higher external and internal auditing costs imposed by SOX.
- Adjust the membership of the board of directors and its committees so as to ensure they will be compliant with SOX and the relevant stock exchange listing standard. Because recruiting new qualified directors can be time consuming, while asking nonqualified individuals to step down can be a delicate task, this process can be quite difficult.
- Increase director compensation and take on additional directors and officers (D&O) liability insurance so as to help attract qualified independent directors.
- Rotate on to a new lead auditor.
- Establish the requisite tone at the top, in which the auditor works for the audit committee rather than management.
- Put into place the procedures and software platform necessary for the CEO and CFO to be able to provide the certifications required by SOX § 302 and § 404.
- Adopt appropriate policies relating to financial officer ethics, conflicts of interest, whistle blower protection, document retention, loans to officers and directors, officer

stock trading, internal controls over financial reporting, and so on.

- Establish a disclosure committee with primary responsibility for reviewing and approving all SEC disclosure filings.
- Review disclosure controls to ensure that the disclosure committee and other responsible managers receive timely and complete information.

In general, most lawyers and investment bankers advise that companies planning an IPO need to be SOX-compliant at least six months prior to the IPO. They also advise that the SEC review to ensure full SOX compliance likely will add two or more weeks to the registration process.

A particular area in which companies preparing to go public often need improvement is their ability to document the adequacy of their internal controls for purposes of § 404. Once a company is required to comply with § 404, it must be able to provide documentation offering reasonable support for management's assessment of the effectiveness of internal control over financial reporting. In particular, the company must be able to document:

- How significant transactions are initiated, authorized, recorded, and disclosed
- How transactions flow within the company with an eye toward flagging areas in which material misstatements could occur due to either mistakes or fraud
- The controls the company has implemented to prevent and detect fraud
- How the company conducts the period-end financial reporting process
- How the company safeguards assets

By the way, most of this advice applies not only to companies considering going public but also to closely held corporations seeking to be acquired by a larger company. A publicly held acquirer that must itself comply with SOX will be disinclined to acquire a business that will create SOX-compliance problems for it. Accordingly, many financial advisors, such as Dick Kilgust of PricewaterhouseCoopers, advise that whether "a private company aspires to an initial public offering, registering for public debt, or one day being acquired by a public company," it should voluntarily become SOX-compliant at the earliest possible date.

Nonprofits and Closely Held Businesses

Only two of Sarbanes-Oxley's provisions apply directly to non-reporting corporations, whether they are nonprofit organizations or closely held businesses:

1. The protections for whistle blowers
2. The prohibition of destroying, altering, or falsifying documents so as to prevent their use or discovery in any official proceeding

Because of the strict criminal sanctions and civil liabilities created by SOX for those who fail to protect whistle blowers from retaliation, it is essential that all nonreporting business companies and all nonprofit entities—no matter how small—adopt written policies of the sort we've discussed in earlier chapters, ensure that top management vigorously enforce those policies, and make clear to all supervisory employees that misconduct will not be tolerated. Likewise, all nonreporting business companies and nonprofit entities must establish a confidential and anonymous mechanism for employees and other stakeholders to report any problems with the entity's financial management.

As for the prohibition of document destruction, it applies to any closely held business or nonprofit corporation that is potentially subject to any form of federal investigation or litigation, including tax, bankruptcy, and other criminal or civil investigations of violation of federal law. Accordingly, all such entities should put into place written document retention policies and communicate those policies to any administrative personnel who handle the entity's books or records. The policy should specify the period for which documents are retained and procedures for destruction of documents older than the required retention period. Education of personnel handling documents is critical to prevent accidental or innocent destruction in violation of the established policy.

Beyond these two areas, nonprofit entities and closely held businesses are not required to comply with SOX, but consider the following: Does your organization have independent board members whose oversight of the organization would be strengthened by the establishment and maintenance of corporate governance best practices? Do you deal with lenders or other financing sources who will want assurance that the organization's financial statements are accurate? Are there other organizational stakeholders with a need for assurance that the financial statements are accurate? Do you risk loss of financing, customers, or membership if fraudulent practices were to be disclosed to the public? If any of these questions is answered in the affirmative, your organization should consider voluntarily complying with key SOX provisions, especially those relating to audits and financial reporting.

CONCLUSION

SOX: An Assessment

We live in an era of instantaneous response. We enjoy instant communication by phone, fax, and e-mail, instant punditry in the blogosphere, and instant books on every scandal du jour. After the Enron scandal erupted, when Congress was desperate to be seen as doing something—anything—about corporate governance, we got insta-legislation: the Public Company Accounting Reform and Investor Protection Act, popularly known as the Sarbanes-Oxley Act (SOX). Unfortunately, Congress was in too much of a hurry for very much in the way of serious cost-benefit analysis. Instead, they threw a bunch of ideas into a single basket and rushed it into law so that angry investors would blame somebody—anybody—other than Congress for the stock market bubble's bursting and the corporate governance scandals.

Now the business community, the SEC, and even Congress are waking up to a basic fact: SOX is costing us a lot more than anybody anticipated. Talk of regulatory relief is in the air, although there are signs that the relief on offer from Washington will prove less extensive than the business community hopes.

In any case, having legislated in haste, Congress is now repenting at leisure. Whether or not their repentance leads to significant relief, the costly debacle should stand as a cautionary tale the next time Congress wants an instant response to some new scandal.

The Unanticipated Costs of SOX Compliance

As an investor, I don't want my portfolio companies spending a dollar on "good corporate governance" unless doing so adds at least a buck to the bottom line. I don't have any voice in how much to spend on corporate governance, however. Instead, those decisions are made by the board of directors and top management. Unfortunately they have strong incentives to overinvest in compliance.

Why? The answer lies in the incentive structures of the relevant players. Who pays the bill if a director is found liable for breaching his federal or state duties? The director. If the director has adequately processed decisions and consulted with advisors, will the director be held liable? Unlikely. Who pays the bill for hiring corporate governance consultants, lawyers, investment bankers, auditors, and so on to advise the board? The corporation and, ultimately, the shareholders.

Suppose you were faced with potentially catastrophic losses, for which somebody offered to sell you an insurance policy. Better still, you don't have to pay the premiums, someone else will do so. Buying the policy therefore doesn't cost you anything. Would not you buy it? Unfortunately, that's precisely the choice SOX gave directors and senior managers.

The most costly statutory provision appears to be § 404, which requires inclusion of internal control disclosures in each public corporation's annual report. This disclosure statement must include: (1) a written confirmation by which firm management acknowledges its responsibility for establishing and maintaining a system of internal controls and procedures for financial reporting; (2) an assessment, as of the end of the most recent fiscal year, of the effectiveness of the firm's internal controls; and (3) a written attestation by the firm's outside auditor confirming the adequacy and accuracy of those controls and procedures.

The most troubling aspect of the dramatic increase in compliance costs is that those costs are disproportionately borne by smaller public firms. For many of these firms, the additional cost is a significant percentage of their annual revenues. Indeed, for those firms operating on thin margins, SOX compliance costs can actually make the difference between profitability and losing money.

Having said all that, of course, we must acknowledge that SOX—even § 404—has had some beneficial effects. First, the basic process of identifying and testing controls is widely believed to have led to improvements in such basic internal controls as revenue recognition, reconciliations, and safeguarding of assets. Second, many companies have substantially modernized their financial processes in response to SOX. The days when WorldCom's financial processes could break down because much of the accounting process was still being done with paper and ink are over. As SEC commissioner Cynthia Glassman observed in a May 2006 speech, "I have no doubt that internal controls are better at many companies, and this is important for investor protection. In addition, Section 404 has caused some companies to streamline their business processes, implement better IT systems, improve documentation of their internal controls and eliminate redundancy." Third, while there are recurring costs, those costs have begun to slowly decrease and should continue to drop as companies more fully implement state-of-the-art information, communication, and monitoring procedures. In that same speech, Commissioner Glassman stated that "total Section 404 compliance costs declined more significantly in year two by as much as 31% or 44%, respectively, for smaller and larger companies."

In sum, Sarbanes-Oxley has done much to improve corporate governance, but the costs have been high. The task for the SEC and the PCAOB going forward is to retain those benefits, while offering appropriate regulatory relief that would help American business comply in the most cost-effective manner.

A Last Word

Instant solutions rarely prove satisfying, as anyone who's ever suffered through a cup of instant coffee knows. Instant legislation is no better. By rushing SOX into law, Congress and President Bush sacrificed the American economy at the altar of short-term political gain. It's time for them to go back and grant the SEC clear authority to provide carefully crafted regulatory relief, especially for the small firms that have disproportionately suffered from the unanticipated costs of complying with SOX.

GLOSSARY

Accelerated filer A reporting company with a float of at least $75 million but less than $700 million. A large accelerated filer is a reporting company with a market float of $700 million or more. A nonaccelerated filer is a reporting company with a float of less than $75 million.

Accounts receivable Amounts owed to the corporation for goods or services.

Adverse opinion An opinion by an auditor stating that the audited company's financial statements do not fairly present the financial position, results of operations, or cash flows in conformity with GAAP.

AICPA The American Institute of Certified Public Accountants, which pre-SOX was the private-sector body with principal responsibility for establishing generally accepted auditing standards. Its regulatory functions have now largely been assumed by the PCAOB with respect to public companies.

AMEX American Stock Exchange.

Articles of incorporation The most important of the corporation's organic documents. Each state corporate statute sets forth the minimum provisions the articles must contain. Among the important provisions commonly found in corporate articles are the number of shares the corporation is authorized to issue, the name and address of the corporation's registered agent, provisions relating to division of shares into classes and series, and limitations on the liability of directors. In most states, filing articles of incorporation meeting the statutory requirements is the sole act necessary to create a corporation.

Assets Tangible or intangible property owned by the corporation, expected to generate future economic benefits. The balance sheet carries most assets at their historical cost (what the corporation paid to purchase them), less any accumulated depreciation. As such, the values reflected on the asset side of the balance sheet often bear no relationship whatsoever to the assets' actual fair market value. Current assets are those expected to be converted into cash within the longer of one year or the company's operating cycle (the time it takes to create inventory, sell it, and collect cash from the sale).

Includes cash, inventory, and other highly liquid assets. Fixed assets are illiquid assets, such as land or equipment.

Audit An examination of the financial statements of an issuer by an independent public accounting firm.

Audit committee A committee (or equivalent body) established by and among the board of directors of an issuer for the purpose of overseeing the accounting and financial reporting processes of the issuer and audits of the financial statements of the issuer.

Audit partner The lead (or coordinating) partner of the accounting firm who has primary responsibility for conducting or reviewing an audit.

Audit report A report prepared following an audit performed for purposes of compliance by an issuer with the requirements of the securities laws and in which a public accounting firm either sets forth the opinion of that firm regarding a financial statement, report, or other document, or asserts that no such opinion can be expressed.

Auditor Public accounting firms registered with the Public Company Accounting Oversight Board and persons associated with such firms who conduct audits.

Authorized shares The number of shares the articles of incorporation authorize the corporation to issue.

Authorized but unissued shares Shares that are authorized by the charter but have not been sold.

Bonds Unsecured long-term debt securities.

Bylaws A corporation's bylaws are its internal operating rules. Other than certain provisions that must be contained in the articles of incorporation, most of the corporation's internal affairs will be governed by the bylaws. Virtually anything may be contained in the bylaws. Among the important provisions commonly found in bylaws are: the number of directors, whether the board of directors is staggered, provisions for calling shareholder or board meetings, and the like.

Certificate of incorporation This term is sometimes erroneously used as a synonym for the articles of incorporation. The certificate of incorporation is delivered to the incorporator by the secretary of state's office when the articles of incorporation are filed. The certificate evidences the corporation's existence.

Certified public accountant (CPA) An individual possessing a credential from a state authorizing the holder to practice as a certified public accountant in that state.

Charter Another name for the articles of incorporation.

CEO Chief executive officer. Typically the CEO is the highest-ranking executive officer of the corporation. In many companies, the CEO also serves as chairman of the board of directors.

CFO Chief financial officer. The top financial officer of the company, with principal responsibility for financial planning, risk assessment, and financial disclosures.

CLO Chief legal officer. An emerging title for the top legal officer of a company (the older title for which is general counsel).

Classes of shares A class of shares is a type or category of stock. Thus, common stock is considered to be a class of stock. Preferred stock would be another class of shares. Multiple classes must be authorized by the articles, which must set forth the number of shares of the class the corporation is authorized to issue and the class's basic rights.

De facto corporation If a defect in the incorporation process prevents the business from being treated as a de jure corporation, but the promoter made a good faith effort to incorporate the business, and carried on the business as though it were a corporation, some courts treat the firm as a de facto corporation. The state may contest the existence of the corporation, but nonstate parties who transact business with a de facto corporation may not hold the firm's promoters or investors personally liable for the firm's obligations.

De jure corporation A de jure corporation is a true corporation: a legal entity that has been validly formed by complying with all statutory requirements. The term is also sometimes used for corporations that substantially complied with the statutory requirements for incorporation but failed to comply with some very minor technical requirement. In the latter case, neither the state nor nonstate parties may contest the corporation's existence.

Debentures Secured long-term debt securities.

Depreciation An expense charged against fixed assets representing the asset's gradual wearing out. Because most fixed assets, except for land, wear out and lose value with the passage of time, accounting principles require the periodic conversion of a fixed asset's cost (carried on the balance sheet) into an expense (reported on the income statement).

Directors Although shareholders nominally own the corporation, they do not control it. Instead, control of the firm is vested in the board of directors, a body of individuals elected by the shareholders to manage the business.

Dividend A pro rata distribution of the corporation's assets to shareholders. A liquidation dividend occurs when the firm dissolves and has assets remaining after all other claims have been satisfied. The residual assets are distributed pro rata to the corporation's shareholders as a final dividend. Cf. *stock dividend.*

ESOP Employee stock ownership plan.

Financial Accounting Standards Board (FASB) A private-sector entity that sets accounting standards.

Financial statements Tabular information about an entity's economic resources and obligations at a point in time, the results of its activities during a particular period, and its sources and uses of cash during that period.

Foreign corporation A company incorporated by a state or nation other than the state in question. All states allow foreign corporations to do business within their borders, and virtually all apply the state of incorporation's law to corporate law disputes involving either foreign or pseudo-foreign corporations.

Form 8-K A periodic disclosure statement that must be filed within fifteen days after certain important events affecting the corporation's operations or financial condition, such as bankruptcy, sales of significant assets, or a change in control of the company.

Form 10-K The annual report filed with the SEC by reporting companies. Contains full audited financial statements and management's report of the previous year's activities. It usually incorporates the annual report sent to shareholders, but also includes extensive additional disclosures.

Form 10-Q A quarterly report filed in each of the first three quarters of the year. The issuer does not file a Form 10-Q for the last quarter of the year, which is covered by the Form 10-K. Form 10-Q contains unaudited financial statements and management's report of material recent developments.

Generally accepted accounting principles (GAAP) The standards constituting defined accepted practices for the preparation of financial statements. The FASB has principal responsibility for defining GAAP.

Generally accepted auditing standards (GAAS) The standards governing how audits are to be conducted.

Goodwill Because of name recognition, brand loyalty, and a host of other factors, a corporation is often worth far more as a going concern than the sum of its assets. In most cases, the company's balance sheet doesn't reflect this additional value. If the company is sold as a going concern for more than the fair market value of its assets, however, the purchasing company will enter the difference on its own balance sheet as goodwill.

Incorporator The individual responsible for signing the articles and delivering them to the secretary of state. If the articles do not name the initial members of the board of directors, the incorporator also holds an organizational meeting to elect the initial directors and to adopt bylaws.

Internal controls For purposes of the CEO and CFO certification rules under SOX § 302, internal controls are the controls and procedures of a company that are designed to ensure that information required to be disclosed by the company in the reports that it files or submits under the Exchange Act is recorded, processed, summarized, and reported within the time periods specified in the SEC's rules and forms. For purposes of the § 404 certification, internal controls are the processes the company uses to ensure that its financial statements comply with GAAP and are free from material misrepresentations and omissions.

Issuer Used in connection with sales of securities to refer to the corporation that originally sold the securities.

Junk bonds High-yield, high-risk corporate bonds frequently used to finance takeovers.

Liabilities The corporation's debts and other obligations. Current liabilities are those coming due within one year and likely will consume current assets. Long-term liabilities are those that are not expected to consume current assets, such as debts not maturing for several years.

Management discussion and analysis (MD&A) The section of a reporting company's quarterly or annual report providing a narrative statement of the information necessary to provide investors with an accurate understanding of the company's current and prospective financial position and operating results. The three required elements in MD&A are the results of operations, liquidity, and capital resources. MD&A must include the potential effects of known trends, commitments, events, and uncertainties.

Material information Information that there is a substantial likelihood that a reasonable investor would consider in deciding how to act.

Material weakness A significant deficiency, or combination of significant deficiencies, that results in more than a remote likelihood that a material misstatement of the annual or interim financial statements will not be prevented or detected. In turn, significant deficiency is defined as a problem with the company's internal controls that adversely affects the company's ability to initiate, authorize, record, process, or report external financial data reliably in accordance with generally accepted accounting principles such that there is more than a remote likelihood that a misstatement of the company's annual or interim financial statements that is more than inconsequential will not be prevented or detected.

NASD National Association of Securities Dealers.

NASDAQ National Association of Securities Dealers Automated Quotation system.

NYSE New York Stock Exchange.

Nonaudit services Any services provided to an issuer by a registered public accounting firm, other than those provided to an issuer in connection with an audit or a review of the financial statements of an issuer.

Notes Short-term debt securities, usually unsecured.

Off-balance-sheet transaction Contractual arrangements that include certain guaranteed contracts, retained or contingent interests in assets transferred to an unconsolidated entity, derivative instruments classified as equity, and material variable interests in certain unconsolidated entities.

Officers The corporation's most senior employees, who are usually responsible for running the corporation on a day-to-day basis. A corporation's officers typically include its president (or chief executive officer), one or more vice presidents, a treasurer or chief financial officer, and a secretary.

Outstanding shares The number of shares the corporation has sold and not repurchased. A corporation may not have outstanding a number of shares greater than the number of authorized shares. If the board of directors wishes to issue a greater number of shares than the articles authorize, it must ask the shareholders to amend the articles to increase the number of authorized shares.

Primary market The securities market in which a corporation sells shares to investors.

Promoter In the broadest sense, the promoters are those individuals actively involved in organizing the corporation. In this outline, the term is used more narrowly to refer to persons who purport to act as agents of the business prior to its incorporation.

Pseudo-foreign corporation A foreign corporation that has most of its ties to the state in question rather than to the state of incorporation. Many Delaware corporations are pseudo-foreign corporations. They are incorporated in Delaware, but most of their operations are located in one or more other states. In virtually all states, there is no significant legal difference between a foreign and a pseudo-foreign corporation.

Public accounting firm An entity that is engaged in the practice of public accounting or preparing or issuing audit reports for reporting companies.

Public Company Accounting Oversight Board (PCAOB) A private-sector, nonprofit corporation, created by the Sarbanes-Oxley Act of 2002, to oversee the auditors of public companies in order to protect the interests of investors and further the public interest in the preparation of informative, fair, and independent audit reports.

Qualified opinion An auditor's opinion stating that the audited company's financial statements in general fairly present the company's financial position, results of operations, and cash flows in conformity with GAAP, but qualifying that statement by noting one or more areas in which the financial statements fail to do so.

Registered public accounting firms Public accounting firms registered with the Public Company Accounting Oversight Board.

Reporting company A corporation or other issuer that is required to register one or more classes of its securities with the SEC under the Securities Exchange Act and, accordingly, becomes subject to the act's periodic disclosure requirements.

Revenue recognition An accounting principle referring to when revenue is counted and thus reported.

Sarbanes-Oxley The Public Company Accounting Reform and Investor Protection Act of 2002 was signed into law by President Bush on July 30, 2002. The act imposes corporate financial reporting and disclosure requirements, including correcting adjustments, additional information on related entities, CEO certification of financial results, and rapid disclosures of material changes in financial condition.

Secondary market The securities market in which investors trade stocks among themselves without any significant participation by the original corporate issuer of the shares. The New York Stock Exchange and the American Stock Exchange are well-known, highly organized, and thoroughly regulated examples of secondary markets.

SEC Securities and Exchange Commission.

Self-regulatory organization A private-sector organization granted statutory responsibility to regulate its own members. Examples include the New York Stock Exchange and the National Association of Securities Dealers (NASD).

Series of shares A series of shares is a subclass of stock. Thus, the corporation might have a class of preferred shares that is divided into series. All members of the class will have some preference over the common stock, but each series may have different rights and preferences from the others.

Shareholder A person or legal entity who owns shares.

Shareholder's equity The difference between the corporation's total assets and its total liabilities. As the corporation's residual claimants, shareholders are entitled to the proceeds of this account upon liquidation. In legal capital terminology, it consists of capital and surplus. Capital is the total par value of all outstanding shares or, in the case of no par stock, the amount designated by the board of directors as capital. Surplus is shareholder equity over and above the corporation's capital.

Shares The units into which the ownership interest of a corporation is divided. Subject to certain exceptions, shares carry two basic rights: (1) voting rights, which allow their owners to elect the corporation's directors and to vote on certain other matters; and (2) economic rights, which entitle their owners to a pro rata share of dividends and, in the event of liquidation, any residual assets remaining after all other claims on the corporation have been paid.

SOX The Sarbanes-Oxley Act of 2002.

State of incorporation Virtually all U.S. corporations are formed ("incorporated") under the laws of one of the several states or territories. The state in which the articles of incorporation are filed is known as the "state of incorporation." The founders of a company are free to select any state as the state of incorporation; they need not select the state in which the company is currently doing business. Selecting a state of incorporation has important consequences, because corporate law matters usually are governed by the law of the state of incorporation, irrespective of where the dispute arose or the residence of the other parties to the dispute.

Stock Sometimes used interchangeably with *shares,* but also used in a more technical sense to refer to the corporation's aggregate outstanding shares, as in the phrase "a share of corporate stock."

Stock dividend A distribution of the corporation's own shares to its shareholders without consideration.

Treasury shares Shares that were once issued and outstanding, but have been repurchased by the corporation. The Revised Model Business Corporation Act (RMBCA) has eliminated the concept of treasury shares (which had importance mainly for purposes of certain accounting conventions), so that reacquired shares under the RMBCA are simply classified as authorized but unissued shares.

Underwriter An investment bank that specializes in selling securities to investors on behalf of their issuers. In a best-efforts underwriting, the underwriter acts as broker—that is, an agent for the issuer/seller—to distribute the securities, with the issuer paying a commission of 1–2 percent on sales. This form of underwriting is predominately used for new, speculative equity securities or below investment-grade debt offerings. About 5 percent of public offerings fall into this category. In a firm-commitment underwriting, the underwriter acts as a dealer (a principal). The underwriter purchases securities from the issuer and then resells them to the public. Firm-commitment underwriting accounts for about 90 percent of all public offerings.

Underwriting syndicate The issuer selects a lead underwriter who is generally responsible for conducting the offering. The issuer and lead underwriter jointly settle on the type, form, and nature of the offering. The basic terms of their agreement are set forth in a nonbinding letter of intent. The two parties then prepare and file the initial registration statement. Once the registration statement is about to become effective the issuer and the lead underwriter enter into an underwriting agreement setting forth the final, binding terms of the transaction. The final offering price is set on the day before the registration statement becomes effective. While the registration statement is being prepared, the lead underwriter assembles an underwriting syndicate of other investment banking firms. The members of the syndicate become parties to the agreement among underwriters, which sets forth the terms of their relationship. Syndicate members will sell part of the offering directly to the public. The remainder is sold to retail securities dealers who join the so-called selling group and who in turn resell the securities to their customers.

Unqualified opinion An auditor's opinion stating that the audited company's financial statements present fairly, in all material respects and in conformity with GAAP, the company's financial position, results of operations, and cash flows.

Warrant A type of option issued by the corporation, whose holder receives a right to purchase securities of the corporation (usually common stock) at the price and on those conditions specified by the warrant.

INDEX

About the Author

Stephen Bainbridge is a professor of law at UCLA, where he teaches Business Associations (i.e., agency, partnership, and corporation law), Unincorporated Business Associations, and Advanced Corporation Law. In past years, he has also taught Corporate Finance, Securities Regulation, Mergers and Acquisitions, and seminars on corporate governance. He has previously taught at the University of Illinois Law School (1988–1996), where the Class of 1990 voted and presented him with the Best Instructor Award; the Harvard Law School as the Joseph Flom Visiting Professor of Law and Business (2000–2001); and at Aoyama Gakuin University in Tokyo (1999).

Bainbridge has written more than fifty monographs for legal journals, including such leading publishers as the *Harvard Law Review*, the *Virginia Law Review*, the *Northwestern University Law Review*, the *Cornell Law Review*, the *Stanford Law Review*, and the *Vanderbilt Law Review*.

He's also written a number of legal texts, including *Agency, Partnerships & LLCs* (2004); *Business Associations: Cases and Materials on Agency, Partnerships, and Corporations* (2003; with Klein and Ramseyer); *Corporation Law and Economics* (2002); *Agency, Partnerships, and Limited Liability Entities: Cases and Materials on Unincorporated Business Associations* (2001; with Klein and Ramseyer); and *Securities Law-Insider Trading* (1999).

Although much of his writing thus has been of a technical nature, he has developed considerable experience in writing for a general audience in his capacity as a weekly columnist for the TCS Daily e-zine (*www.TCSDaily.com*) and as a biweekly columnist for the *Examiner* newspaper chain. A number of his columns have dealt with various aspects of Sarbanes-Oxley.